The
Many Faces
of You

Revealed with Past Life Regression

Andrew Hillsdon

Copyright © Andrew Hillsdon, 2013

Published by Andrew Hillsdon.

A CIP catalogue record for this book is available from the British Library.

ISBN 978-0-9927488-0-7

Printed and bound in Great Britain by:

Think Ink 11-13 Philip Road Ipswich Suffolk IP2 8BH

Cover artwork and design by Andrew Hillsdon.

Dedication

To Tina.

My wife, my world.

Contents

Introduction

My present life began in 1955 and I was born and bred in Buckinghamshire, an area which had seen generations of my family.

In 1987 my wife and I moved to West Devon, and we now have a beautiful farm which we have developed with nature conservation in mind. We planted 20,000 broad-leaved trees which have now developed into wonderful established woodland, teeming with wildlife.

I have always had an interest in spiritual matters and as a child my character formed in ways which were different to the norm. I have never been psychic, that's my sister's forte, but it has never been a requirement for the work that I do now.

Before my career as a Hypnotherapist and Past Life Therapist, I was a telephone cable engineer and an insurance salesman, hardly the most orthodox grounding for my present vocation, but these previous occupations did teach me some useful skills such as communication and rapport, crucial for therapy. I became a Hypnotherapist so that I could practice Past Life Regression, as it is regarded as a special branch of hypnotherapy, although I actually feel that Past Life Therapy is a discipline in its own right, as it encompasses all things spiritual.

My role? I see myself as a stepping stone, helping others onto their spiritual path and this is the purpose in writing this book - to bring to you a detailed insight into this fascinating world. As, to understand who you were will help you to know who you are and, if you wish, to know who you will be - as well as taking a journey into the past, you can just as easily explore the future.

Any of the students who have taken my courses will tell you that they found the information easy to understand and written in a jargon-free plain English style. This book will be the same.

By the time you have finished this work, you will have a good understanding of past and future life exploration and therapy, along with the skills to regress yourself. There will be many spiritual matters discussed and all I ask is that you keep an open mind.

The topics covered are not necessarily my own views or beliefs and have been gathered from research, experience and many conversations. I never impose my ideas upon anyone nor do I judge others for those they adopt. I am not at all comfortable with these self- appointed so-called gurus and I never wish to be regarded as one. The best way for each of us as we travel our spiritual path is to take a brick from every wall, and build our own. Accept only what feels comfortable for you at this time as none of us have all the answers.

Chapter One

The Past Life Journey

I opened my eyes and that wonderful gifted lady guiding the meditation circle was staring right at me. She knew it had all gone a bit weird, I thought to myself, but to be honest I had no idea what had just happened.

There we were, a handful of like-minded people sitting in a circle in our cosy little thatched cottage, just visualising whatever we were being instructed to do, but while everyone else was exploring crystals I found myself floating away from a crashed aeroplane.

This was my first past life experience. When a person meditates they connect with the greater part of themselves. Some call it the Higher Self, others the soul. A hypnotherapist calls it the subconscious, the part of us that carries all the memories of our whole existence. I see now that my subconscious had to provide a bit of a nudge in the direction of a whole new occupation, that at the time I knew nothing about. My life plan was designed for me to become a past life therapist, but at that time I was in a very different industry, and those older readers may be able to identify my job if I tell you I was the man from the Pru.

She knew. That lady sitting across the circle from me knew what I had experienced and she confirmed it when I tried to omit this oddity during the little report we each gave after the meditation. "There's something else isn't there?" She said with all the knowledge and wisdom of a guardian angel. It's just as well I didn't deny my meditation had gone pear-shaped otherwise I wouldn't be sitting here now telling you about it.

She explained to me that I had regressed briefly to a past life and this was all I needed to embark on my new journey of research and discovery. This was before the internet so it was quite a task to find out about past life regression.

Around the same time, my cousin Nick, more than a cousin, the closest thing I have to a brother, found a couple of books about past lives, totally unaware at that time of my own developing interest. Nick is always full of energy and enthusiasm and wanted to have a go at regressing my wife and me into a past life. Another nudge from the universe - what are the chances of someone so close to me suddenly having an interest in something neither of us had ever heard of only a few months earlier. There is a word for these universal coincidences - synchronicity. And that is probably the biggest word you will find in these pages, I am not here to thrill you with my literary skills, I haven't got any.

Nick was very good - he tried his amateur hypnosis on me and soon confirmed my original experience as I found myself flying an old-fashioned biplane in World War One. I was German. Taken to the last day of that life I experienced the terror of bullets hitting the engine, causing it to explode into flames, more bullets tore into my left knee. The horizon disappeared as my 'kite' took a nosedive towards the ground. I knew my time was up, no parachutes were used by pilots in those days. I felt the fear.

So that was the first glimpse into one of my many past lives. I explored that life further, both with Nick and through my own self regression and I found out my name, the type of aeroplane I flew and how many others I had shot down. I took on an arrogant persona during the regressions into that particular life, quite different to how I am in this life.

This story was told to illustrate the fact that there is more than one way to discover previous lives. The main way is by using hypnosis so let's see exactly what that is. Let's start with a big word misconception - here's one: how much honey does a single bee produce in its lifetime? The answer will be found later on in the book. Here's another: "Three, two, one, you're back in the room." No it's nothing like that, you don't fall asleep, you cannot be forced to act like a fool and you remain fully aware of your actions. It is merely a relaxation technique which allows you to focus your mind, it is a natural everyday occurrence. Any time that you are so engrossed in something that you become slightly oblivious to your surroundings, you are in a light form of hypnosis. Reading a book is a good example or daydreaming - you are doing it right now in fact. Just look up from this page for a couple of seconds … there, did you notice how it took a split second to register your surroundings? Just then you snapped out of hypnosis.

People never really feel hypnotized even though they expect to 'go under' because in reality there is no 'under' to go. The feeling of hypnosis is relaxation while focusing the mind. Later you will learn how to take yourself into self - hypnosis but first I'm sure you will want to know why hypnosis is needed to explore your previous lifetimes.

There is a part of us that holds all these memories, that's pretty obvious. Normally we can't remember our past lives, so there must be something we have to do to allow us to access this locked away chunk of our psyche. This storage space in our mind is called the subconscious, or unconscious or Higher Self, or our soul - let's call it Cuthbert for all it matters. It is the greater part of us and it holds a complete record of our whole existence. What a lot to fit in the brain I hear you say. I never said it did, all that data would soon short-circuit if it had to be kept there by little electrical impulses and miniscule chemical changes.

No, I personally believe that the brain is just a converter to change thought into action. Sorry to the men in white coats in their labs with test tubes in hand!

The subconscious has these memories and they can be accessed and retrieved from wherever they are stored by slightly altering your state of consciousness - going into hypnosis.

It is usually understood that the hypnotic state allows us to sneak past the conscious mind, the bit of us that we are aware of and actually thinks. We can then meet the subconscious sitting there behind it. Quite a logical and mechanical concept, but knowing the universe, I'm sure it is much more complicated than that - more likely to do with frequencies and vibrations. It doesn't matter, the point is that it works, so let's not get too involved about the theory, you want to get to the fun bit, after all why do we need to know how a jumbo jet works to enjoy our exotic holiday?

Now the subconscious, Cuthbert, whatever, functions a little differently to the conscious. For a start it doesn't question, filter or rationalise and it has no ability to fabricate or make things up, it just is, like a huge database of experiences and wisdom waiting to be tapped into. It stores memories in a different form too, in visions, feelings and emotions by whatever our five senses record. It is a little vague about accurate dates and names, but that's how memory works. Try to recall your first day at school, think about how it felt, but can you remember the date?

The subconscious communicates with us in a special part of our mind where it can project past life memories and feelings. So what is this weird and wonderful hidden space within us? Our imagination. Go on, look it up in the dictionary and you will find that one of the explanations illustrates that it is a part of your mind where you can see images. Not necessarily where you make things up, because when you are hypnotised the subconscious is dominant and it cannot make things up.

So hypnosis is a state of being deeply relaxed and using your imagination.

Just about everyone can remember their past lives, the only restriction being themselves. There is nothing like the doubt of it working to stop it working. One or two struggle because they work too hard at it and cannot seem to grasp the simple concept of using their imagination, they say they see nothing. How hard can it be to imagine nothing? Go on, have a try - imagine nothing, think of nothing, oh and especially try very hard not to think of the colour blue.

Those clever clogs who think they have won because they didn't think of the colour blue because they were concentrating on the colour red should remember that I said think of nothing.

I have mentioned meditation once or twice and it needs to be discussed as it really is just a form of hypnosis. Others will disagree, but I would say that it is hardly any different at all. If you really want to separate the two you could say that with meditation you are led from outside, guided by whoever is running the circle (or whatever), you are told where to go. With hypnotic regression, although you are basically guided by a therapist the journey comes from within, guided by the subconscious.

The sort of meditations I am discussing are the ones where you visualise. Actually I don't like the word visualisation, it suggests that you have some wonderful cinema screen inside your head and you can just sit back and watch. No, you have to imagine and work at it. Visual type meditations, sometimes called pathway meditation, provide a guided journey in the mind where you have the opportunity to connect on a higher vibration with the spirit world, meet spirit guides and angels, connect with the natural world with its little elves and divas, climb hills, explore caves and get symbolic messages and guidance You can work with energy, fine-tuning yourself, or channel it for healing. Regular meditation launches you on a spiritual path and you can become intuitive, clairvoyant, psychic and sometimes slip into a past life. I love it when I get a new client for Past Life Regression who meditates because I know they will be able to regress very quickly and have a wonderful vivid experience.

Hypnotic regression and pathway meditation are so similar that it is fair to say that Past Life Regression is a blend of the two.

The first time you try to meditate it is really difficult to concentrate and you might get very little out of it. Practice is the key because it is a learning experience for your mind. You are awakening new parts of your soul which have been dormant, in a way, so it takes time and focus. It is exactly the same with regression into previous lifetimes and at the beginning of the first session you try you may be a little disappointed. By the time you get to the end of the session you will see that things have improved. Practice, practice, practice, just like with anything we do. An Olympic gold medallist is not perfect from the word go, they need to practice.

The reason I am stressing this point is to save you from being despondent should your first past life exploration be a little disappointing. It may not be, most of my clients have a great first session, but at least you know it will get better with practice.

Some of the top past life therapists are not Hypnotherapists and provide past life meditations. "Explore past lives without hypnosis" they say yet the methods they use are exactly the same. In fact, let's worry no more about hypnosis - it's just a label, it is what happens when you close your eyes, relax and use your imagination.

Oh, did I say? It's perfectly safe as well. I sometimes hear things like "I'm scared because the bloke down the pub says it's dangerous and I'll get stuck in a past life". What twaddle! If I ask you to remember what you had for lunch last Friday, would you get stuck dreaming of a ham salad? I don't think so. Regression is just a clever way to recall memories, that's all, so it's perfectly natural and safe.

Every Past Life Therapist, or if you prefer to use an Americanism: Regressionist, has a different style when they take their subjects into their past lives, but there is a strict structure that most follow.

Here are the steps:

1. Close eyes
2. Breathing exercise
3. Relax the body
4. Imagine surroundings
5. Descend steps
6. Find a 'safe place'
7. Enter a past life

In step four your imagined surroundings take the form of a journey of some sort and a theme is employed. This gives uniformity and familiarity which helps to build confidence in the past life explorer. My usual theme takes the form of a garden, as it is an easy thing to remember and has all the elements to stimulate the senses, but you can choose from numerous visual journeys such as buildings, lifts, tunnels and even time machines. Once the garden has been explored a little in your mind's eye, steps are then descended which symbolically guide the subject into a deeper state of relaxation. The area at the bottom of the steps has some form of resting place, usually a reclining garden chair, and this is known as the safe place. It is somewhere of familiarity to return to if you get lost or wish to rest.

Within the parameters of the garden theme, access to previous lifetimes is via a row of doors built into a garden wall, each one taking you to a different period of time within all the past lifetimes that can be explored. Each door is a year apart and the further you go down that path, the further back in time you go. This will be elaborated on in greater depth in chapter 8.

There are many reasons to have a Past Life Regression, apart from just seeing who you were. We can carry issues into our present lifetimes which have their roots in events experienced in earlier incarnations. For instance there are many souls incarnated at present whose past lives were in the concentration camps during the war under the Nazi regime. Many were gassed to death and now they are seeing therapists to deal with all sorts of symptoms such as breathing difficulties, fear of enclosed spaces, or weight problems because of the malnutrition back then. People also come for regression to see if they had shared a past life with someone they are close to in their present life, others just want personal proof of reincarnation. Then there are those characters we bump into who look like they are stuck in the past, the eccentrics dressing in a style and fashion more akin to their grandparents. When a 20-year-old man feels comfortable in a trilby hat, perhaps he is still carrying the energies of his past life back in the 1940s or 50s. This can go a stage further too in some people. What about the individuals who are absolutely fascinated with a particular historical period? Perhaps they build model ships like HMS Victory and read everything they can about sea battles and strategies. Others may have a fascination with the English Civil War and join re-enactment societies such as The Sealed Knot. If they were to seek regression to help them understand their obsessions I think there is a good chance that they would find a past life relative to their favoured historical period.

At some time in our life we may meet someone for the first time and feel completely at ease with them, as if we have known them all our life. This could be to do with Soul Mates which we will look at later. The reason I mention this phenomenon about a feeling of familiarity is that it can happen in places too. Occasionally someone may find themselves in a town that they have never been to before and yet it all seems so recognizable and they can even predict what is around the next corner. The fancy name from this occurrence is Triggered Recall meaning that something that has been picked up by one our five senses triggers a past life memory. This doesn't mean that by going into the garden and smelling a rose you will be transported back into Edwardian England as you take a little air before luncheon, but certain stimuli can evoke certain feelings and vibes, even a déjà vu moment. If this keeps happening, you may totter along to your friendly local Past Life Therapist to see if there is an answer. Similar to triggered recall is spontaneous recall where past life feelings and memories surface of their own accord, sometimes in the form of flashbacks or intense daydreams. Children do this in that golden time between learning to talk and forgetting these past memories, a little window of opportunity somewhere around 3 to 5 years of age. They come up with little gems like "My last Mummy made much better cakes", or pointing to a tiny birth mark and saying "That's where I was shot"... How many potential documentable cases have been lost because parents didn't pick up on what is happening?

Another example of why people seek regression is the curse of Far Memory, a very rare phenomenon but for the person who has it, a real nuisance. With far memory, an individual (I played with saying sufferer here) has a total recall of a past life, usually only the one. It is there all the time in their thought processes, sitting side by side with all their present life memories. When you regress a person with Far Memory, you seldom get past their alter ego. There is always a good reason to have Far Memory and I assume that it is part of a life plan, either to clear a name that has been wrongly accused in a past life or sometimes to sort out some unfinished business. Author and therapist Brenda Harwood has this phenomenon and has written books about her experiences. Here is a passage provided by Brenda in the form of an introduction to her second book:

"The reason why I have decided to write this second book *I Live Again* is I felt the rest of my story needed to be told, that of my former life as Christopher Marlowe. I understand that there are those of you who do not believe me or understand what has happened to me.

What happened to me in 1978 changed my life forever. It has not been an easy road to travel and believe me I have made many attempts to walk away from it. I have tried to block out what was coming through, but it continued even though I put all my notes away locked up in our garage. To be brutally honest the thoughts became stronger by being more and more intense so I had to give in.

The Many Faces of You

Having the knowledge that I was Christopher Marlowe made me realise there was no escape for me. I have now accepted even though many years as passed that I have to live with it and do my best not let it take over my life. I have learned to do this by keeping my other interests going, such as drawing, knitting and socialising. I know if I did not keep a tight rein on things he would take over as his persona is far stronger than mine. This is also another reason why I became a past life therapist as I have a understanding of what is going on and am able to empathise with those who may come to me with similar issues.

I am lucky I suppose as I have had a lot support from my family and friends. They have listened to what I have had to say and some have themselves experienced past life memories. My husband has also studied past life regression. Unlike most people who have been regressed I was not and never have been because this was not necessary as I had what is known as 'spontaneous recall'. This is where you recognise a situation and you answer in the first person like I did when I said in my first book, "I didn't die like that" when it came to the scene where Christopher Marlowe allegedly died in a tavern brawl in Deptford. This scene from the series Will Shakespeare opened up what has being laying dormant for many centuries in my inner being for the time was right for it to come forward.

Other instances where there is happens is when I hear a song or watch a film or play about the Sixteenth Century I start to remember things that happened in this period. I even remember everyday life experiences that bring memories flooding back into my mind. For this reason I always carry a pad and pen with me when I am out and about. Often I see it happening like a film in front of my eyes and sometimes my persona changes to that of Marlowe's. I know when this is happening because my voice and manner change so I have been told by family and friends but I have learned to control this over the years. Fortunately though I have no memory of what occurred.

These changes in my personality occur more so when I am near places where Marlowe lived, such as London and Canterbury. It even happened when my husband and I were on holiday in Verona and Padua these being places where Marlowe lived while spying for the Queen and in exile.

To put this book together I have had to go through many pages of hand-written words and phrases and trying to make sense of what I had put down. My life has not been without pain and suffering for I have had three operations and many deaths in my family so I have had to deal with all of this which I put down to 'life' and get on with putting together this next book.

The strange thing is I never knew about Christopher Marlowe or his existence. I was always good at history, art and religious education at school (some of the subjects Marlowe may have excelled in) but never made it to A-level standard. I accept that this is what I have to do and that is, write what he has to say. I have tried myself in meditation to see who I was before Marlowe and after but I am not able to do this as he is always there and I become him.

Andrew Hillsdon my tutor for past life therapy told me that in this life I have to finish what I have started and that is why I as Marlowe have returned to set the record straight. He is not happy being made into a plaster saint, he was human like everyone else and had human failings. There were times when his life was not his own, especially if he wanted to live. So he had to do what he was told and be controlled. This was something he did not like for he was a man who would like to be in control of his own life.

I call him my 'other self' as I feel that I am two persons in one.

I sometimes find it very hard to write about what I see but if I do I record it and get my husband to typeset it for me. Living with this day-to-day is difficult sometimes even though I have lived with it since 1978 and I am now 62 years old and we have been married for over 34 years. The strange thing is when the far-memory happened to me we lived at house number 39 and I was 29 years old. Since then the numbers 39 and 93 have followed me and my husband around. Kit (Christopher Marlowe) says he is the phoenix rising from the ashes as is supposed death was at 29 years old and the year was 1593. Is this a coincidence or fate, I will leave up to you to decide.

Love and light, Brenda."

Finally, the main reason that people seek regression is to understand where their intense recurring dreams come from. These dreams feature vivid elements of a previous lifetime and I believe that this is the subconscious trying to sort out some imbalance.

Let's now look at reincarnation. You don't have to believe in this concept in order to experience a Past Life Regression. It happens anyway, but this book is not being written to prove its existence or otherwise. Personally I do believe in reincarnation and the majority of people who have chosen a spiritual path do also. That doesn't make it true or false and I'm not sure how much it matters really because Past Life Regression is an experience to help you along on your path, offering enlightenment and healing.

There are one or two other theories for those of you who would like a choice, or are reading this book to dissect it for a report in a sceptics' magazine. Here are a few:

The Many Faces of You

Inheritance. This theory suggests that we inherit these memories through our DNA from our ancestors. Actually I do give that suggestion the time of day because there is something in the idea that certain behavioural traits do transfer to future generations. When an individual, adopted at birth, grows up and tracks down their natural birth parents they may recognise certain similarities in habits and mannerisms. So yes, I believe that many things are associated with the genes. How else could we have those primeval basic natural instincts? This concept does fall short though when it comes to the complex mechanics of bodily incarnation because if you choose to find out about your past lives and have many regressions you will find that you have been every colour, culture and creed that there is. I am sure that if you find that you were once an Australian Aborigine, that's hardly going to be connected genetically to an upper middle class family line. You're more likely to have been your own Granny.

Another alternative theory to reincarnation is the idea that you are tuning in to discarnate souls, mind reading those in spirit while they sit on their clouds playing their harps. You could be I suppose, but then you would be taking on a persona that you do not recognise with different character traits. In regression you do recognise your own habits and behaviours, so the spirit mind-reading idea falls a little flat.

How about the sceptics favourite - it's all fantasy you are just making it up. If this is true then there are a lot of good guessers out there, as no end of case studies have been researched and documented, especially so these days thanks to the internet. Facts that no-one could possibly know can be verified very easily. Again, it doesn't really matter that much if we were just making it all up and there are many who think this during their regressions. As long as it has therapeutic value and some sort of cure is provided then it has benefit, fantasy or not.

Most of the world's major religions accept reincarnation, except Christianity, in the main, plus one or two others. In fact here is a bit of news which will rub a few million Christians up the wrong way, there were references to reincarnation in the Old and New Testaments. In A.D. 325 the Roman emperor Constantine the Great, along with his mother, Helena, deleted references to reincarnation contained in the New Testament, then another go was had by the Second Council of Constantinople who got together in A.D. 553 and declared the concept of reincarnation as heresy.

Emperor Justinian belonged to this group that wanted reincarnation outlawed. Justinian gathered together all the decision-makers of the church, a very powerful bunch where anything agreed upon and adopted by them become a way of life for everybody. Emperor Justinian ordered them to discuss a matter that was not part of the original agenda, the teachings of a person called Origen, known as Origenism, who died in the year 254 AD. During the discussion, Emperor Justinian, who at that time was in bitter conflict with the Pope, proposed fifteen condemnations of the teachings of Origen, one of which was the idea of pre-existence of the soul - reincarnation. As expected, all the proposed condemnations were approved by the council of Constantinople led by Emperor Justinian. Despite the fact that the Second Council of Constantinople on reincarnation, in 553 AD, was unpopular and rejected in most quarters, its negative effect is today biting hard on this generation because most Christians of today do not know what transpired in Constantinople in respect of the knowledge of reincarnation, which used to be an undisputable belief among the Christians of that time. Since there was no subsequent official pronouncement to annul the decision of the Emperor Justinian-led council, the word reincarnation was carefully left out when "The Book of Laws", the original scriptures, was being packaged into the present-day Bible. Since the minds of many present-day Christians have been conditioned not to accept or believe anything that is not in the Bible, the knowledge and concept of reincarnation gradually faded away.

Therefore the fact that the word reincarnation is not directly mentioned in the bible does not mean it doesn't exist. What you have in the present day Bible is what a group of people felt should be in it, those teachings that the church was not comfortable with were carefully left out.

I am not saying this to anger anyone, I'm stating facts that can be easily be researched. The Bible is still full of references about reincarnation such as the phrase 'born again' and 'rebirth' but you would have to read it with your 'I believe in reincarnation' hat on to see the clues and let's face it, if you are on a spiritual path and believe in reincarnation then perhaps you may not want to read the scriptures in the first place. Again, everyone has a choice and I never judge anyone or challenge their beliefs or impose my views on them. No one has all the answers so take what you want and leave the rest. Yes, I know I've said that before. One final point of interest and I can't remember where I read this, so I may be wrong, this business about Justinian and his earlier peers removing reincarnation from the Bible is taught in Theological college!

As a therapist and trainer I get many questions about reincarnation and regression and here are a few:

Question: How many lives have we had?

Answer: Probably thousands, occasionally hardly any at all. There are all kinds of existences apart from this three-dimensional planet we call Earth. There are different dimensions, energies, planets, planes, so we don't always find ourselves choosing to occupy a lump of meat evolved from apes. If we like the third dimension or we create unfinished business, then we'll be back.

Question: How long do we spend in the spirit world in between incarnations?

Answer: Surveys I have conducted give an average of 13 years. With my own previous two lives it was 12 years and 9 years respectively. You must remember that time is a concept of this material world and the rules are different in other spirit realms, therefore the gap between lives can range from seconds to millennia.

Question: What if I find out that I was a horrible person in a past life?

Answer: The idea of life is to experience and to do that thoroughly we return again and again to gain as many experiences as possible, by being every sort of person and enacting every role. So we have been horrible people because we have chosen to be, we have all been killers, we have all been killed. And it is just as likely that we have chosen lives where we have had the experience of being kind loving and unselfish. There is no good or bad, no judgement from others, just experience. So embrace whatever you find out about yourself in regression and see what you can learn from it.

Question: Do we reincarnate as animals?

Answer: I personally have not encountered this in regression, apart from the unusual one set in far pre-history in chapter 6. There have been cases documented though and I feel that we would not reincarnate as animals now, but we may have many years ago before our modern bodies had evolved to accommodate us.

Question: How far back can you go?

To the beginning. Actually it is quite difficult to define what the beginning is as it all becomes a bit bizarre. There is a whole chapter dedicated to far pre-history later in this book.

Question: Why do we reincarnate?

Here are a few suggestions:
Evolution - We reincarnate in order to experience and evolve. I think I can safely state that without creating too much discussion.

Karma - We reincarnate to balance out our Karma. The laws of cause and effect – what we do to others, we must have done to ourselves. The more you look into the understanding of the laws of karma the more complex it appears. It is seldom as simple as 'an eye for an eye'. It would appear that we can have karma with individuals, groups of people, places, and even whole countries.

As always, the universe is probably too complicated for us to comprehend completely.

Entrapment - We reincarnate because we are stuck here. This premise suggests that we are enslaved within the low vibration of this third dimensional planet, and only when we can all raise the vibration of our 'collective consciousness', through balance of karma etc, can we then escape the cycle of rebirth.

Addiction - We keep coming back because we are addicted to life. It has been said that we keep longing to return to the flesh over and over again because there just isn't any substitute for the pleasures and sensations of the third dimension.

God's Will - Imagine that there was nothing. Just nothing, no stars, no planets. This nothing was occupied by intelligence, a universal consciousness that was all-knowing. But knowing what? What is there to know about all that nothing? Well, nothing.

So this ultimate intelligence had to do something then in order to know more than nothing. So it thought into existence energy and then when it knew everything there was to know about energy, it started playing around with this energy and discovered that if it compressed it, it would form into solid matter. Brilliant! Lots more to learn now. Eventually this matter evolves into stars and then planets. Great, even more knowledge to gain. The physical world, awesome! So this wonderful perfect consciousness knew even more but there was still something missing. Experience. The intelligence needed to experience to be complete. Then it would have enough to think about, living in nothingness was mind-numbing but now things are looking up. It then decided to split part of its consciousness into tiny pieces so that they could interact with each other and thus feed this need for experience. These tiny pieces are called souls.

Hopefully you now have a good understanding of what Past Life Regression is all about, and in chapter 8 you can learn to self regress. It must be stressed that self regression is purely for curiosity and exploration, just a quick insight to who you were. When it comes to therapy, which we will have a look at later, I recommended that you see a reputable therapist. Details of how to find one are in the back of this book.

The Many Faces of You

By the way, a bee produces $1/12^{th}$ of a teaspoon of honey in a lifetime. Respect the bees.

Chapter Two

The Spiritual Side

By its very nature Past Life Regression embraces all things spiritual, it goes beyond the simple premise of a belief in reincarnation.

Once we enter the complex world of the subconscious we are, in some ways, connecting to that greater part of us that remains in the spirit world. It is understood that when we return to Earth only a small fraction of our whole being joins up with the flesh, so to speak. This part of us is known as the Lower Self and it is our consciousness, the thinking, experiencing part. The bigger part which stays in spirit is known as the Higher Self and although the two parts remain linked, most of us feel removed from that connection. It is all to do with energy and vibrational frequencies. I could get technical here but I'll try not to. The three-dimensional world, planet Earth, runs at a very low vibration and that is what makes everything solid because if you break down any object, whether animal, vegetable or mineral, to its tiniest component, you will find that it will be a photon of light, a particle of energy. In a dense, low vibrational environment all these particles squash very closely together and form solid matter.

When we incarnate and become part of this dense, low resonating dimension, our vibrational frequency plummets in order to balance with our surroundings. Therefore we lose our connection with the higher spiritual frequencies which, in turn, stops us from being able to remember the fantastic existence we have just come from. This is why we don't normally remember our previous lifetimes.

When we meditate or become hypnotised our vibration starts to rise, different brainwaves are produced and we start to connect to our Higher Self, or subconscious, or that other chap. Our past life memories are stored there in these slightly higher frequencies so then we can remember them.

I have the feeling that as we reincarnate and go through this vibrational downturn it is a gradual transitional process, as I am sure that a new born baby has a full recollection about where he or she has just come from, they just can't tell you about it. Even by the time they get to four or five years old, many still have fragmented memories of their past lives but soon the dense and negative third dimension closes them down.

This is why I regard Past Life Regression as a wonderful springboard for those wanting to go on to a spiritual path in life. Through meditation and hypnotic regression, people can reawaken their connection with the spirit world.

As I have already stated, practice is key. The more often you meditate or regress, or chant or indulge in numerous other spiritual practices the more you raise your vibration. And the higher the vibration the more connected you become and this, in turn, brings new gifts for some of us such as intuition and psychic ability.

Occasionally people are born with the gift of seeing, being psychic from the word go, this very often runs in families. Is this because the genetic make-up of their particular family line provides flesh bodies which allow vibration at a higher level?

Within the spiritual fraternity it is common belief that we are all slowly evolving and our vibration is raising collectively. Many advanced high-frequency souls are coming back to Earth at this time in order to make this happen. They are referred to as Light Workers or Star Children. To survive, the Earth needs to raise her own vibration and this can be helped by the collective positive energy of everyone. A steady old job though, it did quite well back in the 1960s but the drudgery of life soon dampened it down again. The Earth needs to ascend, which means she has to shift her vibrational frequencies up a gear and if we could all lay down our guns and hug the person next to us, she would do it overnight, I'm sure.

Here's a question. How often do you glance at your digital clock and it is showing 11:11? Apparently this is some sort of sign from the spirit world, a wake-up call. The symbolism of 11:11 is complex and it is too far away from Past Life Regression to discuss in this book but it does have a connection with this vibration raising. There, now I have passed on the wake-up call.

It is important to be aware of this vibrational upsurge because it has an effect on you when you regress. In meditation many work with the energies within their bodies, raising the frequency. Within the framework of the physical body there are energy centres, or hubs. They are called chakras and there are seven main ones and numerous smaller ones. A practised meditator can increase the vibrational frequencies of these energy vortexes by focusing on them. Some will perceive this energy as spinning, like a Catherine wheel, others will see them as a flower bud gently opening, and as this happens, the frequency of their whole being increases, enabling them to connect to their Higher Self.

Chakras need to be cleansed because they can hold on to negative energy in one form or another and spiritual healers can work with them, removing the bad energy and creating balance.

The more spiritually advanced we are, meaning that we have practised methods which raise our vibration, the more our chakras respond to any altered state of consciousness, such as hypnosis. Therefore if a client with a raised vibration has regression, their chakras will open. Here then is the reason for waffling on about these energy centres, open chakras can make an individual vulnerable to attack.

Who are the attackers? Entities, malevolent spirits, lost souls, aliens, anything within those other dimensions that might have a sinister agenda. Open chakras act like beacons in the dark and they attract all sorts, like moths to a flame.

Many of us carry entity attachments and there is a healthy industry out there to provide a service to remove them. It should really be done by experts because these nasty beings can not only be stubborn but they can also hide. People who carry entities can have all sorts of symptoms such as voices in the head, emotional imbalances causing depression and outbursts of anger.

"But you said it is perfectly safe to regress." I hear you scream. Well it is as long as you use protection. No, not that sort. By protection I mean putting up a barrier to stop the spirits attaching. All you have to do is think of yourself surrounded by a light in which you are cocooned. Your therapist may automatically do this for you as a matter of course or you can do it for yourself just prior to hypnosis. Alternatively you can incorporate this protection into the initial induction into hypnosis and in chapter 8 when you learn to self regress you will be shown a way to do this.

Energy is what it is all about. It is what we are made of, it surrounds us in the form of our aura and every thought we have creates subtle changes in our energy field.

Just as we have energy centres joined by meridians, energy lines throughout our body, so does the Earth on a much bigger scale. She has chakras, Uluru (Ayers Rock) in Australia and Glastonbury Tor are probably the most well-known. These are joined up by the Earth's equivalent of meridians, ley lines, and they can be easily dowsed, or just felt by the more spiritually sensitive amongst us.

Talking of ley lines, there are a couple of very strong ones which run from the east coast of England down to the South West. One is called the Saint Michael line, the other the St Mary line. The interesting thing about these lines is the places that are located along them. Along the length of the Saint Michael line are many churches called the Church of Saint Michael, and with the Saint Mary line, yes, you've guessed it, that one goes through Saint Mary's churches. These lines go straight through the middle of them. Christians knew a thing or two back in the day.

It's all to do with energy and the manipulation and balancing of this energy is an important part of the therapy side of Past Life Regression and hypnotherapy. Not many clinical hypnotherapists will do energy work as it is really down to the more spiritually aware past life therapist.

Energy exchange happens to everyone all the time, often in a good way, but just as often in a bad way. We all carry energy in one form or another, within us and around us. This energy is fluid and swirls around us and stretches out in all directions. Science can't really detect it, therefore it can't measure it. It could be regarded as a form of electromagnetic energy like the strong field you get around high-voltage cables and equipment. Our energy is of a higher frequency and although it cannot be quantified by science, it can be felt by all of us.

Places carry energies as well. I am sure you have been into a room in an ancient property and felt an atmosphere. As we are beings made of energy we have the ability to feel these atmospheres. We can feel ley lines, a nice vibe in a stone circle, and the dark depressing feel of a haunted cellar where there has been a history of mass murder.

Every time you connect with a person whether it is through direct conversation or by just getting one of those looks, we are exchanging energy. Do you know anyone who talks at you so much that it leaves you drained? Perhaps you know others who leave you buzzing and energised. There are the givers and the takers, some stealing your energy with intimidation and loving people that give freely making you feel happy and content.

Love is one of the strongest energies and when you are in love, you are sharing positive energy with someone you are very close to and receiving theirs back. Positive energy is great as long as it is balanced and passes both ways. It is the negative energies that need healing and balancing.

Imagine a past life scenario where there was a young man who was absolutely head over heels in love with his beautiful wife. He doted on her and lived his life to make her happy. One day he came home and found a note that she had left him and run off with his best friend. How would he feel? Devastated of course, emotionally numb and totally drained of energy. His heart aches and he feels suicidal. In one way or another she has stolen his energies, leaving him with a broken heart. He had given everything in the form of love energy and she had taken it away. So now we have an imbalance - she has something of his and probably feels great with all the excitement of eloping. No guilt, no remorse. This is an example of how karma can form between two souls, it is the imbalance, the unfinished business and there has to be a way to balance it out, so we reincarnate again to reverse the roles perhaps to regain the taken energy. In another life our two characters may make a contract together, prior to incarnation, where they create a plan to play the opposite roles.

When you encounter such an experience in Past Life Regression, there are ways to regain that energy and sometimes we may just need a fine tuning if it is shown that in other lifetimes that karma has already been balanced. Once a few regressions have disclosed the details of the imbalance, a meeting can then be arranged whilst in hypnosis. The client can be the man with the broken heart in this example, and he can invite the soul of this past life estranged wife to visit him for a meeting. An exercise can then be done where the energy is returned to its rightful owner and balance and harmony is restored.

If too much energy is taken from a person then something else may happen. A soul can be damaged and a part of it can actually split off and become lost. Very often the missing soul part becomes stuck in the physical location where the massive energy drain took place. Perhaps this has something to do with haunted places, where ghosts seem grounded and just act out a repeating pattern of activity, oblivious to anything. This could be a broken off soul fragment, lost in the wilderness. I'm not saying this is fact but it is food for thought. The name of this phenomenon is soul fragmentation and there is a therapy in Past Life Regression called soul retrieval which is used to identify when and where the fragmentation took place, and then to go and retrieve the lost bit. If a soul incarnates with a missing fragment, the individual could lead the whole of their life in response to the mislaid part of them, always with the thought that there is 'something missing' in the back of their mind.

The Many Faces of You

Soul fragmentation can occur in a person's present life understandably, and the reason this happens can be the same as in previous lifetimes. I had a case a few years back where a client had some of her closest family on the other side of the world, in Australia. On one of her visits over there she stood in a beautiful park which overlooked the bay in Sydney, the Opera House within view. She had become quite attached to the country, not least because of her family being there. Here in this park she had a moment of absolute bliss, smelling the flowers, feeling the sun, knowing her family was nearby and then reality struck as she remembered that she was due to fly back to the UK the following day. It hurt, she felt sick to her stomach and really didn't want to leave. This jolt caused soul fragmentation and she left little bit of her behind in this park. When she was home she developed a yearning to return to Australia just living her life for her next visit, she even looked into emigrating. This was caused by her need to reunite with her missing soul fragment which had created such a void in her life. In therapy we identified soul fragmentation as the problem and by using some unusual techniques including astral travel, she was able to transport her energy, her soul, to the other side of the world and collect her fragment. In hypnosis she was able to fly to that park and when she arrived she could see herself standing there looking wistfully out over the harbour. All she had to do then was invite that other facet of herself to join her and then fly back home.

All sorts of emotional trauma can cause soul fragmentation and it very often occurs because of an act of injustice in a past life. Perhaps a so-called witch was burnt at the stake and all she did was care for people. A part of her soul could feel so angry, so betrayed, that it may choose to stay behind and in a bizarre sort of way, seek justice. The lost part of her stays there at that location where the burning took place. In her soul's present incarnation she may choose to voice this subconscious rage by perhaps writing a book about the plight of witches in the olden days. She may also have an obsession about the country in which the witch hunt took place and visit as often as she can, having an affinity with some particular small town or another. What she is doing is seeking her lost soul part.

So, souls can fragment through emotional trauma and mostly remain behind at the geographical location of the original event. But not always. Fragments can also attach to other souls. We are back to the 'he stole my heart situation'. Yes he may well have done and the swine still has it. Great, all we've got to do now is find the right one out of the 6½ billion people on the planet and ask for the part back - simple! Luckily, the universe works in incredible ways to make sure the right individuals get together. In my mind, there is no such thing as coincidence and everything that happens is part of a master plan of unimaginable complexity designed to arrange the synchronicity required for souls to join up and sort out their indifferences. What are the chances of you going on holiday, meeting someone you then fall in love with, moving out there to be with them and then having a Past Life Regression that reveals you have shared many other lives together? No, it was meant to be, your fortnight in Ibiza with your mates was part of your highly organised pre-incarnation life plan.

High speed travel can upset the energy system too. Our flesh bodies are not really designed to be hurled through the air six miles off the ground at five hundred miles an hour. I have a theory that air travel actually stretches our energy field, the aura, and it has to cling on to stay with us forming a sort of plume behind us like a loose scarf on a motorbike. It can take a while to fully return and rebalance and I am wondering if this is a contributor to jet lag. Even on short haul flights travellers can feel drained.

Next time you travel, whether by plane or car or train or running very fast, try this little exercise once every half an hour or so. Close your eyes and call back your aura by imagining it being pulled into you. You will arrive at your destination feeling much more refreshed than you would have done otherwise.

Another problem that can happen with all this tearing around the planet at high speed is soul fragmentation. Those who travel a lot, spending a large chunk of their time with their aura stretched hundreds of miles behind them can end up leaving little fragmented pieces of themselves all over the globe. I dealt with a case of this once, the lady I saw was very unsettled not knowing what she wanted out of life, not being able to decide where to live in the world. Whilst she was in hypnosis I asked her to imagine seeing herself in a special full length mirror with a digital gauge on top of it. I instructed her to look beyond her physical reflection and observe herself as an energy form and tell me if there were any parts of her that looked as if they were missing. As an extra indication she was guided to look at the gauge, this read as a percentage and I asked her to tell me what it read. The gauge would measure her wholeness, the higher the percentage the more complete she was. She started off at 60%, so there was 40% of her energy which was scattered to the four corners of the planet. I won't go into the technicalities of the therapy but it transpired that the missing bits were in five different locations and we recovered these parts piece by piece until she registered 100% on the gauge.

Yes, I know I have digressed from the subject of Past Life Regression, but so do therapy sessions. What starts off as a desire to see who you were can end up in astral travelling around the world collecting missing parts of yourself.

Sometimes, however hard you try with a client, you just can't access a past life and it's not about a particular individual's inability, it's just not on their subconscious agenda. The subconscious can object quite strongly sometimes and snap a subject straight out of hypnosis if we are not doing what we should be doing. I had one such case who approached me for Past Life Regression. Michelle was on a spiritual path, doing very well in her development circle to become a medium and she also attended a spiritualist church. She wanted to experience a Past Life Regression and perhaps get some answers for her presenting issues. Her partner died very suddenly a year before and it devastated her, turning her life upside down. She had never really got over her grief. She also had blocked tubes within her sinuses which caused hearing problems and many courses of medication had failed to remedy this. She also carried a lot of shoulder tension. We attempted our first visit to a previous lifetime, but it was not all that clear. Her visualisation was great and she relayed her observations in good detail, but none of it made sense. She found herself in an old-fashioned street with those Tudor style black and white houses where the upper level overhung the ground floor. Cobbled streets and other details followed. The problem was her, she didn't belong in that scene, dressed in leather strap sandals and a short white toga- style tunic, she was more likely to be an ancient Greek. There was a further complication in that she could only observe herself from the outside, from the third party perspective. She could not become that person she was seeing. Eventually I got her to feel how this body felt, but even then she could feel nothing, it was ethereal as if she was a ghost in that scene. To the left of the scene there was nothing at all, it was just dark and dropped away to nothing. This was proving to be a symbolic scene, these occur occasionally when a subconscious has a different agenda. All we have to do is try to work out what it is trying to say.

Or we can ask it, which I did.

The answer was: "From the outside looking in". Great, that's all right then. Thanks, as clear as mud. Needing a little more than I had gleaned so far I had Michelle leave that scene and once back in the garden asked her to reflect on what had happened so far, allowing words of wisdom to just flow into her mind. This is what she said: "I feel I have always been waiting for something, everything is in the future. I think I've missed a lot of my life, no involvement or belonging."

She then mumbled something about sensing a very strong smell of coal and soot and promptly snapped out of hypnosis. This is where it is crucial to have a therapist who can decipher cryptic messages offered by the subconscious mind. We had a chat about what had happened so far and I suggested that the significance of the coal and soot smell was important, a clue. With Michelle concentrating on the smell we returned to the row of doors. The next part is an example of a phenomenon known as interlinking where the subconscious shows us similar events from different lifetimes, mixing them together and creating more confusion. First of all she was in a past life by a large open fire, characters standing around in period clothes. On moving forward to a significant event, she found herself listening to an argument, people again standing by an open fire. She was hiding away, covering her ears, switching off. With the detail that followed she was clearly distressed and appeared to be in a different time period and, on leaving this scene, I asked her observe the date on the door, it was the year of her birth in her present life as Michelle. So all along her subconscious was screaming at us that it was a 'this life' issue it was here to deal with. After a chat we returned to the hypnotic state and I asked her subconscious to confirm whether the issue relating to Michelle's blocked ears was in her present life or a past one. It confirmed what I suspected, Michelle's present life, when she was four.

With this case one thing led to the next and whilst having a meeting with her four year old self to encourage her to cease the habit of covering her ears when she wanted to cut out unpalatable experiences, I thought while we were there I would ask the grieving part of her character to come forward as well so we could find out why she wasn't putting her grief to rest. Another clue was given to me here because that part of her manifested as an ethereal ghostly image, not solid. To me this represented something not whole, showing perhaps that this part of her, which connected to the loss of her partner, had fragmented. All we had to do was find her missing soul fragment and reconnect to it. To help her find the missing part of her we first started with the mirror exercise, the one with the gauge above it, then it was time for a bit of astral travelling, which involves a process whereby subjects are instructed to leave their body, float up into the atmosphere and relocate to the spot where the missing soul part is stuck. She found herself in the cottage where she had spent those wonderful four and a half years with her now sadly departed partner. We recovered her fragmented energies and then she returned. One more attempt was made to regress to a past life to see if she had incarnated previously with her partner but once again the subconscious was having none of it. She snapped out of hypnosis again. We had done enough anyway and she felt exhausted after doing so much.

The above case is shown here to demonstrate the fact that you won't always get what you expect from a Past Life Regression session. What started as an interest in past lives, and whether they held any imbalances that affected her presenting symptoms, led to a number of issues needing to be healed in her present lifetime. The four-year-old within her was responsible for her blocked ears, her missing soul fragment contributed to her ongoing grief and the feeling of being slightly removed from everything around her. So where was it missing from? Her right shoulder, so this was probably the cause of the inexplicable excess tension that she had in this area.

Now that we understand a little more about energy, we will now see how all this exchange between people affects our karma. The subject of karma can get very involved. The simple way to describe it is an eye for an eye, as quoted in the Bible, another reference to reincarnation that slipped through the Roman Emperor's net. But karma is very complex. Not only is it about imbalance, it could also be regarded as a useful tool to enable our souls to undergo a wide range of experiences. The simple rules of karma are "Do unto others as they do unto you", whoops, there goes another one, shoddy work, Emperor. In other words, if I stab you in one life you will have to stab me in another. This tit-for-tat seldom happens in such a simplistic way and karma is more likely to be balanced out in much more subtle yet complicated ways. Once an imbalance, or karmic debt, as it is sometimes called, happens it binds two souls together in as much as they will now have to work together when in spirit to devise a plan to come back and balance it all out.

Most often souls who have this bond of common purpose are members of a soul group, which is a collection of individuals, perhaps a dozen or so or many more who have interacted together over many lifetimes, then return time and time again playing different roles and having various tests to try to balance things out. Not every member of a soul group will reincarnate at the same time, maybe just a handful depending on the karma to be balanced.

Within soul groups we find Soul Mates, which are two members of a group who are very close and may reincarnate together more often. Soul Mates have an affinity for one another and the bond between them is very strong. This doesn't mean that they always choose a shared life with a loving relationship each time, again it depends on the karma produced by the ups and downs of their many shared lifetimes.

And then there are Twin Flames. Now here's a complex thing and everyone seems to have a different interpretation as to what Twin Flames are. Mostly it is understood that we all have a Twin Flame and it is regarded as the other half of ourselves, not the Higher Self as such but more of a Yin to our Yang, a mirror image. Normally our

Twin Flame stays in spirit while we are visiting the Earth and very occasionally both halves inhabit different bodies at the same time. It is said that if this happens it means that this particular time is their last in this physical dimension.

This may account for an occasional phenomenon during therapy where a client will tune into another lifetime that is current, in the present, or sometimes just a few years back into regression. There is a clash of dates, meaning that our subject could not possibly have lived that other life whilst living their own. Are they connecting with their Twin Flame?

There are other souls who stay in spirit and still connect to us and these are our spirit guides and guardian angels. They are normally advanced souls, meaning they are of a more evolved higher vibration and choose to remain in the spirit world to help us mere mortals in our struggle through life. Many of our spirit guides have had the third dimension experience, having reincarnated many times. So that we can identify them in meditation or regression they usually appear as one of the people they have been in one of their incarnations. You often hear spiritual people say "Oh, my spirit guide is called Running Water, he is a plumber." No, sorry that was a feeble attempt at a joke, it should have been "He is a Native American Indian." Yes, he may appear as this, but it's not what he is, of course, as he is neither a he nor a she and is pure spirit.

There are many differing opinions about spirit guides. Some say they watch over you 24/7 - yes, even when you are doing that! Others say they come when you call, whether consciously or unconsciously. They can be responsible for those little flashes of intuition or inspiration and will wake you up when daydreaming just before you are about to step out in front of a car.

It is also generally agreed within the spiritual fraternity that our guides change as we develop our spiritual skills through meditation or healing etc. I don't mean that our one guide changes what he or she looks like, no, they actually go on to other duties and are replaced by another being, so we get an upgrade every now and then.

We can also have more than one guide at a time, each with their own particular duties. One may be there to watch over us and keep us safe, while another may help the synchronicity in our lives, by guiding us to souls we need to meet up with.

When you embark on a past life journey, you can actually meet your guide, usually in the garden, building or beach depending on your theme. You may wish to sit and talk with them or have them accompany you on a past life journey, helping you find the right life to explore, then they can assist you in the understanding of that life.

Then there are angels.

Angels are at another level altogether and I guess that there are different levels in the angelic realms. The whole subject of angels can command a book on its own, so it is best for this work to keep it as simple as possible and write about the angels' role in past life therapy.

Angels are becoming more popular all the time and this may be to do with the rising frequency and consciousness of the population. Their role within past life therapy is whatever your subconscious chooses. If, for some reason, you need to meet with and communicate with these very high ranking spirits, then a past life session can be a platform to make that happen. Some people, who are in tune with these angelic beings say that there are specific angels for different tasks and there are, amongst others, past life angels there to help you connect with the inner wisdom gained over many lifetimes. Others heal or protect.

Contact with angels when in hypnosis is not easily achieved by everyone as this is back to the energy subject again. Beings of this order vibrate at an extremely high-frequency compared to ourselves, so only some of us can raise our vibration enough to tune into them. Not that we can get anywhere near to their true frequency, an impossible task for flesh-bound lower selves, but I assume some people can just open up a channel of some sort. For the rest of us an encounter with angels whilst in regression will result in various sensations of colours, energy vortexes and feelings akin to travel sickness. The energy just spins us out.

There are many other types of spiritual meetings that you can have while under hypnosis and a good number of these can happen in the safe place, the chair in the garden, recliner by the log fire or the flight deck of the time machine.

The most important meetings will be with the souls that you have karma with. You first explore your past lives and with the help of your therapist guiding you, the original cause can be found for the symptoms you carry in your everyday life. If this cause involves the actions of others, which it invariably does, then you will have identified the individual who is responsible for your imbalances. Trauma, energy stealing, physical or mental abuse, to name but a few, all create an emotional reaction of some sort or another. The emotional variations that ensue are carried through to other lifetimes, unless of course it is all sorted out at the time. If we could all prevent karma from occurring by balancing our indifferences with people then karma would go out of fashion and we would all evolve much quicker.

This is to do with what is known as Karmic Partners and these are souls that we have had an encounter with during a previous lifetime but are not necessarily a member of our own soul group.

There could be just one instance where a karmic imbalance occurred. As an example let's look at a modern problem of the misfit who has some sort of breakdown and calmly walks into a school with a gun. The poor children that are hit by a bullet are the subject of random bad luck, and the gunman has nothing to do with their soul groups, but a lot of karmic debt has been created. So when the gunman and the pupils get together in the spirit world a karmic contract is worked out so that the gunman has the opportunity to atone for that complete mess he has made of the scholars' life plans. This is where it is hardly ever an eye for an eye, as a child from the classroom is hardly likely to choose a life where he or she would go 'mental' and massacre innocent people. The role of the former gunman could be to help the former pupil to fulfil their original life plan, the one they had all worked out before this madman entered the classroom.

When a life is unexpectedly cut short, causing a carefully orchestrated life plan to fail, think of the number of souls that get affected. It's the Butterfly effect - what a great deal of karma that gunman has created.

If your present life has been planned to sort out the karma that you have just regressed to, then you will no doubt encounter your karmic partner. You may think that sounds all a little too easy, you just regress to some random event and all of a sudden a couple of weeks later up pops the karmic perpetrator in your local pub. Yes, it does happen like that and no, the event experienced during your regression was not at all random. Think how many karmic experiences there must be stored in your past, thousands probably. Remember that the universe works with mind-boggling complexity and you may have been destined to be born as you, be regressed when you are 35 years old, identify your karmic partner in the event that happened 200 years ago, then meet him or her down the pub a week next Tuesday. It happens.

If your lifetime is really well organised you may find that your karmic partner has also chosen a spiritual path and the reason you meet in the pub is because it was a convenient gathering place for the first meeting of a meditation circle. All you need to do then is encourage this person, who is perhaps, 'responsible for your mistrust of the opposite sex', or whatever issue you have, to have a regression as well and see the link between you both. Common knowledge and understanding goes a long way to resolution.

Remember that a karmic partner is a relative stranger, and not a member of your soul group, so this imbalance was a one-off and therefore free of any further complications or compounding. This can be balanced quickly and easily. It is another story with your Soul Mates. Time after time you and your bunch of mates come back to the flesh in numerous guises, your sister was perhaps your lover in your last life together, you produce karma, come back to sort it out, get it wrong, produce more, and so it goes on.

How on Earth do we get to sort this out in therapy? Luckily the subconscious has an understanding of previous lifetimes that have karmic links and if it is a little keen to heal these imbalances it will flit all over the place jumping from one lifetime to another in what seems like a totally random fashion. What it is actually doing is something called interlinking, when it attempts to show us the different lifetimes where attempts to balance one particular karmic debt have been made. Interlinking can be both frustrating for the therapist and confusing for the client. Although the subconscious is trying its best guide you to the imbalances, is not really helpful to have all this jumping around. Stuck here in the third dimension we like things to start at one end and finish at the other, it works nicely with our concepts of linear time. The subconscious or Higher Self is free from such boundaries and the production of a previous lifetime montage makes perfect sense. This is one of the many reasons that most past life therapists use structured themes, a door for this year and another for that. We can then rein in an enthusiastic subconscious and regain some decorum.

What makes a karmic imbalance? To some degree, just about every encounter we have with other beings. Everything we say and everything we do will have a consequence, causing a change in the environment and the people around us. Perhaps, karma is just to do with energy exchange. Let's look at an example.

If a gentleman gives up his seat on the train to a lady to sit down and she gives him a beautiful smile and says thank you, then the energy exchange between them is balanced, it flows both ways and produces no karma. If however the same gentleman got out of his seat and the lady said nothing, ignored him completely and sat in his seat then we have an imbalance. The man will perhaps feel hurt, taken for granted, angry even. He had offered energy freely in the form of a polite and kind gesture, the lady had taken that energy in a cold and selfish way. This could one day compound, as perhaps they may both commute on that train daily. If the same situation presents itself a second time, he may be reluctant to give up his seat, she would expect him to and feel rebuffed when he doesn't. Obviously this scenario is just to show an example of how easily an energy imbalance between two individuals becomes karma, not that my mild example is likely to result in a huge karmic debt causing people to continually reincarnate until they get a hassle-free seat on a train. What it does show is that karma can be big or small and certainly frequent. No wonder we have to reincarnate hundreds, possibly thousands of times to sort it all out.

The bigger picture can soon get very complicated. Going back to my little train scenario, what would happen to the futures of these two people in response to how they acted within those few seconds? This is where we need to explore the concept of parallel universes and the butterfly effect. Let's take the first scenario:

The man on the train offers his seat and the lady is truly grateful as she is not feeling too well and is probably getting a touch of flu. She tells him this and a conversation ensues. The person next to the lady gets up and leaves the train so that man can now sit down. They get on really well and discover while they are talking that they are both single and live in the same town. They both get off the train, he asks her for a date which she accepts. A year later they are married.

In scenario two, she is rude, ignores him and no conversation takes place, so nothing happens. No bond, no romance, no marriage.

Who is to say that both scenarios won't happen? The universe is complex in more ways than we even have the slightest hope to start to comprehend. Perhaps every single action that we do, every little decision that we make can result in ourselves taking the choice of two paths. So what about the other path? What happens to it? Here's the interesting bit, in Past Life Regression you can regress back to that choice, junction if you like, and then choose the other path, the one you didn't actually go down. By doing this you will be able to explore a whole new past life, one you didn't have. It would seem that the subconscious, your soul, your Higher Self whatever it is, holds all the memories of every alternative path and resulting lifetime you could have had. Think of all the different paths there must be. It's got to be infinite.

Our life therefore, the one we are actually living, is the end product of every thought, deed and action we have ever made in our entire existence, all leading to this moment when you're reading this sentence in this book on this day. Just think that if you had a life in ancient Egypt thousands of years ago and you had stubbed your toe on the edge of that huge statue rather than not stubbing it, then perhaps you would never have read this book!

This is all theory, of course, and I am presenting it to help you consider the bigger picture, which could be very big indeed. None of what I write about is fully my view, it is all just for consideration and discussion.

Our soul could be living almost infinite parallel lives and Past Life Regression can help us to explore a handful of the alternatives. Here another interesting twist to the subject, regression in this present life. Alternative paths in our previous lifetimes could ultimately lead to completely different lives upon reincarnation. In our present lifetime, meaning you, here and now, a glimpse at an alternative outcome could be very interesting indeed. Think about it, have you ever wondered what would have happened if you had stood up to that bully at school, or what would have happened if you hadn't fallen out of that apple tree and broken your collarbone? Very subtly, the alternative paths would have taken you into a completely different lifetime. How weird would it be to regress back to the instant something happened and then see what would have happened if you had stood up to the bully or held onto the branch a little bit tighter.

The therapy used to help you see these other scenarios is called the Alternative Outcome Technique and therapists who do this are rare. There is a very good reason for this and it is because I invented it. There may be others out there who claim the same, but in a world of parallel universes, it's bound to happen. I teach the technique in my advanced Past Life Regression course, so only practitioners who have studied this will able to practice my version.

You may be wondering what use this technique is to anyone. As far as past lives are concerned, there may be some therapeutic value in understanding where the karma went bad. In this present life, especially where our memories are relatively complete this can cure the anxiety caused by the 'what if' mind set. If you ever wondered what would have been had you chosen the other option when confronted with a major decision, now you can see. Even if it shows a more favourable outcome at least you'll be free from worrying about it on some deep subconscious level.

Wouldn't it be very useful to be able to make the right decision at the time rather than having to see what could have been in retrospect? What luck, there is another technique to do just that and this one you can try for yourself. It is called the Future Choice Meditation. I use the word meditation as it has a greater element of therapist (or script) led guidance, more like a pathway meditation. You are still in hypnosis, or a meditative state or whatever else it could be called and it is a journey in the mind which starts from the safe place, chair in the garden, the armchair, the shed on Mars, whatever you prefer. For simplicity's sake, I will always use the garden theme as it works for practically everyone, unless of course you have a particular dislike of gardens.

The idea of the Future Choice Meditation is to give you, the mind traveller, the opportunity to see the future outcome of an important decision that you are faced with and it normally deals with two alternatives, but there is no reason why we couldn't have more choices. Again this is a spiritual journey because you are engaging your Higher Self in order to get the guidance you need. Time is fluid in spirit so your future scenarios are all mapped out, rehearsed ready for you to follow.

Under the guidance of your therapist, or if you are doing it on your own, your memorised script which you will see in chapter 8, you leave the safe place, your comfortable reclining garden chair and then go across to a different part of the garden, where you will find a wide pathway. At this point you leave the garden and enter a wood. The path is long, wide and straight. You see, you are imagining this already aren't you - I said that you were in hypnosis when reading a book, didn't I? Anyway, back to the journey. After walking along this track you eventually come to a T-junction and this symbolically represents your choices to make. The track to the left symbolises one of your choices and one to the right, yes you've guessed it, the other choice. At this junction there is a signpost and on the signpost you can imagine words to describe your two choices. For example the sign pointing to the left could be 'emigrate' and the one to the right could be 'stay put'. You can now explore both directions, one way first, then back to the junction and then off in the other direction. This is where the idea of this being a meditation comes in, because what you experience isn't necessarily a perfect vision of the future (we will look at that later on in the book) but a symbolic experience. In our scenario of emigrate or stay put, in one direction you may encounter a rocky road, withering trees, perhaps a steep incline symbolising an uphill struggle. The other direction may put you in a beautiful yacht gliding across a still, smooth lake and that could symbolise plain sailing, meaning it will go very smoothly. In addition to the symbols encountered along the way your therapist may direct you to a resting place where you can be instructed to find a small gift, a symbolic token. Whatever this item is, it will be personal to you and your circumstances, perhaps an empty purse warning you of financial hardship or a lovely gold chalice which usually symbolises wealth.

One direction will be very obviously positive, the other negative, so you will know which path you should choose.

Your spirit guide can accompany you on this journey if you wish and can be very helpful by assisting in the search of particular symbols or the gift. You can also rest a while and discuss the symbolism that you find along each path to help you interpret it.

So if you use this technique now, you won't have to see a therapist in the future for the Alternative Outcome Technique to see what would have been. The Future Choice Meditation is another technique I have personally developed over a period of time so if you approach another therapist for it, they may look at you with a blank expression.

Have you ever seen a ghost? Ghosts are very interesting and the reason this subject is being raised within the context of Past Life Regression is that some people can regress to being ghosts. There appear to be many forms of these wonderful apparitions. Some are regarded as grounded, others come in visitation. In general, I personally believe that ghosts are just spirits that have become Earth-bound. A certain amount of the right sort of energy may be required to take a soul off to the light, our natural home, and it seems that in the majority of cases these wandering souls have become stuck here due to the circumstances in which they died, which deprived them from getting this energy. Very often it is violent or unexpected deaths which keep the spirits upon the Earth plane. Because they are trapped in this low vibration, the frequency is more or less the same as the living, the only difference is that they are not inside a flesh body. Is this why we can occasionally see them, because we are on a similar wavelength?

The ones in visitation may not be Earth-bound, in as much as they are not always at the same location. There appears to be a free will and a greater communication function. They still haven't fully gone to the spirit world though and very often this is because there is unfinished business. For example, they may have had a brief and unexpected death just when everything was going well and a master plan was about to pay dividends. Their sudden demise deprived them of their glory and they feel so annoyed that they can't move on. So we come back to energy again, emotional energy to be precise, and before we go on I would just like to reiterate what was said at the beginning of this book:

No one has all the answers. Take only what feels comfortable.

I put that in here because the theories I am discussing are just that, theories, my own. I am offering a few alternative ideas for discussion, that's all. So these theories about ghosts may all be wrong, who knows, there are many stock explanations out there and what I am trying to do is offer some fresh ones. These work for me because I feel it makes sense.

So, emotional energy and ghosts. As stated, the spirit world vibrates at a much higher frequency and in the natural preparation for death we have the time to adapt as we part from our bodies in a calm and relaxed condition and as we move over to the spirit world, our vibration slowly rises. If, however, we are highly emotionally charged around the point of death, the vibration of our energy is affected by the strong emotions and if these emotions are negative, which would be the case with anger, or terrible sadness, then it can block our energy from rising, thus keeping us Earthbound. So the unfortunate few remain at a low vibration and live in that halfway house, the twilight zone between the third dimension and the spirit world.

There could be other reasons they become ghosts. Remember that a strong emotional trauma can cause soul fragmentation. Could a part of the soul breaking away at the time of an untimely death be a ghost? Would the result of that happening entrap a soul here? I think it could. The sort of ghost that you see as result of this happening is the 'loop tape' one, where you always see it in the same place, repeating the same actions like a stuck record. These sorts are typically totally unaware of the presence of people who are alive and there is no real communication possible with them. Perhaps they are the echoes caused by the lost soul fragments, they broke away and got left here on the Earth plane and just function automatically, repeating the part of the soul's life that these particular fragments were responsible for. One of the many theories for this repeating behaviour is to do with the location and some believe that the energy of the event is somehow recorded in the stone walls of buildings. I can go along with that idea to a point. It is all to do with energy, so therefore a certain place could hold on to energy from the past, especially if there is emotional trauma contributing to it. How this is projected into something that some people can see with the naked eye must be more to do with an individual's sixth sense, they may be affected by this lurking energy which then gives them a visual. Or maybe they are tuning in to one of the other parallel dimensions?

Being a ghost is relatively rare as most of us live quite happily and toddle off to where we should and therapists will have very few clients who regress to being one of these lost souls. The fact that some do regress to a ghost occasionally, and yet are there in the therapist's chair, would suggest that they stopped being a ghost at some point. That might well be the case, but it could be that another aspect of their soul is still being a ghost. It is only a tiny little part of our whole being which occupies the body, the rest stays in spirit, so perhaps we can be in more than one place at a time. If there is a possibility that we are living in an infinite number of dimensions at the same time, what are a couple of extra ghosts?

Here is an interesting case study about a ghost regression and I would like to thank therapist Madelon Geluk for her permission to publish it.

*   *   *   *   *   *

This is just an informal outline of the ghost regression that I have done. The client had seen, at some point, a historical painting of the takeover of the McGuire Castle and lands in Northern Ireland. He had a strong feeling he was present at the time and needed to get to the bottom of it.

The regressions started off with him being a young boy, seven years of age. There is panic all around and lots of people, the whole McGuire clan is rounded up. They are tricked under false pretence and gathered together on the bridge by the river (or lake). Soldiers are forcing people off the bridge now. Bodies are falling on top of each other and drowning.

All of his family. The client cries and shouts, "Oh my God, there is aunty so-and-so and uncle 'B'," very upset, caught up in the horror of it all. "Everyone is in panic".

Forward now and he stands laughing really hard, they are all laughing (all of the dead people). "Ha ha, the bastards (meaning the English) thought they could kill us, but they can't." He laughs for a long time with all his drowned people. The eels are eating many of the bodies, others bloat or float away. He is mock angry with 'our own eels for eating us.'

The whole clan lives on. As a ghost (in his own words) he has insight into the emotions of the living. The English soldiers feel no remorse, but the Bush Soldiers (in the English army) are very upset, they know they have committed an awful unlawful act, killing women and children and tricking people under false pretence. It rests heavily upon their souls.

He is merging with his father now, who was not present and is still alive, walking along, holding his hand. But he realises after a while his father can't see him, because he is a Catholic and thinks that they have all gone to heaven. He laughs some more at that realisation.

All the ghosts hang about and eventually gather on the old path huddling in a tight cluster, the little ones in the middle for protection.

At some point he wants to move on but they hold him physically in the huddle. Eventually they move aside to let him go and then he is out of the centre and leaves, his life as a ghost is over.

My client now claims he feels invincible and immortal.

*   *   *   *   *   *

Let's just summarise the concept of energy. If you break down the human body, you will find it is made up of cells, made up of molecules, each of which have smaller particles inside. You eventually end up with the smallest particle which really isn't made of matter, just pure energy. So we are made of energy.

We can sense energy, send it out and receive it. We can have it stolen and we can replace it by sitting quietly in nature, or we can jolly well steal it back.

Every time we interact with others, energy exchanges, imbalances occur. We may leave these imbalances behind in past lives which creates karma. Does reading this book make you feel better or worse?

Chapter Three

Therapy

Alongside curiosity, the other main reason that people have Past Life Regression is for therapeutic reasons. There are numerous conditions that originate from previous lifetimes and just as many ways to heal them.

It is time for a word of caution. There are many spiritual practitioners around, some are card readers, others clairvoyants, mediums or energy healers and many of them have a go at past lives during the course of their readings. That's all right as far as a little exploration and knowledge of a few previous lifetimes is concerned, after all the methods to do this for yourself are in this book and it's perfectly safe. It is the healing side which could be a problem and one really should be trained and qualified as you never know what these powerful healers are going to stir up. I am not saying that anything they may do is dangerous or foolhardy as all regression work is just an exercise in remembering, but the therapy side is complex and to do the best for clients, people should know what they're doing.

The Many Faces of You

So if you are looking for a therapist, please make sure that they carry the proper credentials. To be sure, have a look on the Past Life Therapists Association's database online as all the practitioners you will find there are fully qualified and recommended by the Association. This was one of the many reasons for setting up the Association as all of the Past Life Regression and hypnotherapy industry is un-regulated, meaning that the government doesn't recognise these disciplines or set any rules. I'm sure there are politics involved here and we may well ask ourselves why the powers that be will not take any notice of a therapy that aids a large number of people wishing to give up smoking with a success rate in excess of 95%, yet will push and promote to the ends of the Earth the nicotine replacement therapy paraphernalia such as patches, inhalers and gums, which only have a measly 6% success rate. These are statistical facts that can be verified. That's it, no more politics from now on.

The other aspect of therapy that makes it complex is the fact that every case is unique and therefore therapists will forever be learning through experience. I often say this to my graduating students: "Your clients will teach you the rest."

All this still doesn't mean it is difficult to learn, as nearly all of it is quite mechanical and most training is script-based, meaning that the therapist reads the written word to induce clients into hypnosis and make the past life journey. There are other scripts for the therapy side to.

Past Life Therapy is not exclusive to the regression fraternity as there are other disciplines which get involved in past life work, whether planned or not. Reiki is a well established form of healing work, concentrating on energies. This powerful technique works on many levels of the psyche and occasionally it will bring a past life issue to the surface. There are a number of ways that Reiki practitioners deal with these imbalances. Many of the students who train with me are practising Reiki masters and teachers and the experiences they have had with clients have sparked an interest in past lives, so they have the desire to learn more about the powerful healing methods used in regression. These two very different therapies dovetail nicely together and complement one another.

Two of the most frequent symptoms that clients bring to Past Life Therapists are fears and phobias. Actually, to be accurate a fear is a phobia and vice versa. If you want to be the pedantic then a phobia is probably the deluxe version of a fear, the top of the range fear with greater power and intensity.

A phobia is described as an irrational fear, something that you are really scared of, but most people are not. Phobias can be very debilitating, restricting and misunderstood. People who see an individual suffering from these irrational fears are quite often impatient and unsympathetic towards them because they just cannot believe that anyone could be afraid of bananas. If they knew that they had suffered a horrible lingering death as a slave in a banana plantation a few lifetimes before, then perhaps they may just be a little more tolerant.

The reason that phobias form, whether in past lives or in our present one, is to do with how the subconscious works and they usually start with some sort of overwhelming trauma. If something happens to us that is so devastating, so unpalatable that we just cannot handle it, then our normal everyday rationalising conscious mind temporarily closes down, switches off, as we go into shock. The conscious mind normally observes, filters, questions and generally makes sense of whatever experience is being presented, that's its job and only this part of the mind does it. If it switches off then it leaves the poor ill- equipped subconscious exposed and there it is, like a rabbit in the headlights facing the traumatic experience head on. Without the conscious mind there to protect it, it just takes in everything that is happening. The distressing incident has been taken in as an irrationalised set of instructions the subconscious works on the principle of a "your wish is my command" mentality. There is also a big chunk of unexpressed emotion involved as well and this all gets shoved in on top of the trauma, unfelt and raw. After a short while the trauma passes and the conscious mind switches on again. The first important thing is that it has not taken on board the experience in any shape or form, it does not remember it, total amnesia sets in and this is why many people have missing parts of their memory after accidents. The word to describe this set of circumstances is called 'repression'. Events are repressed within the subconscious and there they sit and fester. One day, sooner or later, the repressed event and, more importantly, the associated trapped emotions will cause havoc and create symptoms, the most common of which are phobias. In fact a repression can lead to numerous other symptoms such as psychosomatic ailments, anxieties and depression to name but a few and also physical elements, such as aches and pains, asthma and eczema. However, phobias tend to be the most common and let's have a look at a scenario which could lead to one:

Back in a past life a young boy was playing with his brother near a well. It is an old-fashioned hole in the ground, wide and very deep with just a rough crumbling stone wall around it. Their parents have always told them not to go near the well and had put the fear of God into them and woe betide if they disobeyed their parents. But boys will be boys and rebels, especially at that silly age when they think they know better. The young lad's brother starts showing off and climbs onto the low wall on the edge of the well, then despite his sibling's protests he starts to walk around the wall, balancing with his arms outstretched and wearing a big grin. Suddenly a stone on top of the wall gives way and the last thing the boy sees is his brother's expression changing to terror as he disappears. A scream follows then a thump and a splash. The boy just stares, shock having taken over completely, his inner mind in turmoil. Is he dead? Father will kill us, kill me. I can't tell him, I'll say I don't know where my brother is. Then he runs far away, holding his hands over his ears, trying to blot out that terrifying scream. He rests under a tree shocked and numb, his mind going blank, slowly closing down. A few hours later his parents find him curled up in a foetal position, white and shivering. They ask where his brother is, and he genuinely has no idea. Shock has repressed the whole incident, he didn't even know how he ended up beneath a tree nearly a mile from home.

The whole traumatic experience is now repressed and total amnesia has covered it over. The chances are that as he now goes through life he will never remember the day his brother died.

But his subconscious will.

Thirty years later he is walking along a river bank and he sees a young child right beside the river's edge, poorly supervised by his parents who are walking along in front. He freezes and a huge surge of anxiety rushes through him. He has a full-blown panic attack as he imagines the worst, thinking this child will lose its balance and fall into the river. He also gets angry and shouts at the parents, telling them to look after their child properly. His childhood repression has manifested in this very specific phobia, a fear of children near drops where water is involved.

In his next life that phobia will manifest again. It could be any number of circumstances which will cause the phobic anxiety, children on a cliff top, in a rowing boat, even on top of the castle keep overlooking a moat. The phobia will probably evolve, they usually do, to perhaps a fear of heights, a fear of still, deep water, the fear of seeing any unsupervised child.

It is the trapped emotions which have not been experienced, repressed in the subconscious, which cause the symptoms of a phobia In our scenario, not only were there emotions of fear, sadness and loss but also ones of guilt. On some level, although not consciously, there is a feeling of guilt for not having done something positive and getting his parents after his brother's accident. What if he had? Would his brother have survived the incident? In following lifetimes whilst suffering the phobia he (or she in another life) may try to externalise these issues by choosing a career or vocation where child safety products are marketed, such as special covers for fishponds or harness systems with reins to put on toddlers.

So how does Past Life Regression Therapy help to cure these phobias? It can be very straightforward. Regression is the main tool for phobias and many other symptoms which have causes in previous lifetimes. The same rules apply for our present life too. A Past Life Regression Therapist will ask the client to look for the past life where the original cause of his or her phobia originates. They then explore that past life and with some gentle guidance and coaching from the practitioner relive the original event. There may be a degree of reluctance on the part of the client's subconscious to allow this trauma to be re-experienced, it has repressed it once and it really is at the back of the cupboard stuck underneath all sorts. When the event is relived in the mind's eye of our phobic client, the emotion that is associated with the original scene, but was not experienced at the time, can now be felt, and sometimes, boy, is it felt.

As the emotion is experienced and starts to release, it could cause strong feelings in the client and they could do anything from a tiny whimper with a couple of tears, to a powerful outburst. This response to an emotional release is called abreaction and can last a few minutes in some cases before the client settles. Don't worry as these spectacular reactions are very rare, I've only ever had one so kinetic that I was worried that my client would hurl himself out of my therapy couch.

Following abreaction, which in most cases you hardly notice they're so mild, there is a period of time following therapy when the remainder of the trapped emotions purge from the subconscious. This may take a few weeks in some cases. This period is known as catharsis but let's not get too hung up on big words. During the cathartic period, the individual may experience odd bursts of emotion at strange times as the last few residues bubble to the surface. Once all the emotion has cleared, the symptoms of the phobia disappear permanently. The fear of children near edges with water will never be an issue again. The emotion goes, so symptoms go.

There are two main categories of phobia, the simple ones such as a fear of snakes and the more complex ones like the example shown in our 'boy by the well' scenario. There is a certain amount of natural instinct involved in these fears, instincts that have evolved to keep us safe. It is quite natural to have a fear of snakes or spiders, we may have been killed by something in a past life, but when someone visits the therapist because they have a fear of telephones or the colour blue, then you can be pretty sure that it's a repressed incident driving a phobia.

There are other phobias which are not only complex but are also not what they seem. Let's have a look at the fear of flying. If you think about it, what is it about flying that is fearful? Well, crashing I suppose. So it's not a fear of flying at all, it's a fear of not flying. In fact the fear of flying is actually to do with one very important concept: control. It's all about control. There you are, stuck in this metal tube hurtling along at 600 mph and you don't even know who the driver is. I once met someone who was petrified of flying yet was given one of those birthday presents of an hour long flying lesson. He thoroughly enjoyed his experience and he was really good at handling the aircraft - because he was in control. The next time he went on a normal commercial flight he was terrified again!

Phobias that originate from previous lifetimes can be very confusing for the sufferer. It is easy enough for a simple 'this life' phobia of say, the dentist, because there is a fairly sure bet that it started when the child had all those teeth taken out in one go. But when your phobia has no bearing on anything in your life, such as one of polar bears, but not brown or grizzly bears then unless you cotton on to the idea that it's a past life issue then you are going to remain pretty confused. The more bizarre the phobia, as long as it is a fear of a particular individual thing, the easier it is for the therapist to see that it originates from a past life.

Fears and phobias are part of a whole plethora of symptoms that have their causes in previous lifetimes. There are respiration problems originating from drowning, the feelings of sadness when you see the plight of a certain race on a film, physical ailments at the point where an injury once took place, in fact, just about anything.

To allow healing to take place, first you have to find the cause and to do that you have to be guided by a qualified Past Life Therapist. With gentle direction you will be able to home in on the particular life that holds all the answers. Once you experience the original cause of the present day symptoms we then have a starting point for therapy. A good proportion of the healing is automatic - by gaining the understanding of the circumstances which created the original incident emotion is released, sometimes, and knowledge is brought into conscious awareness where it can be reconciled. There are other healing techniques which can be used once the cause has been uncovered.

One very useful technique is called re-framing and what this basically means is that you go back and change something. This may sound a little odd, but it is quite feasible because of the way the subconscious functions. The storehouse of our mind records everything in fine detail, in chronological order, this has to be done I suppose because our aim as living beings is to experience, and there's no point in doing that unless we remember and use that wisdom. Regard the subconscious as a huge DVD or hard drive of the size that makes the one in your computer seem like the equivalent of a teaspoon of the river Nile. This superb recording device does just that, records. No filtering, no censoring, that's already been done by the conscious mind prior to archiving. It follows therefore that if we could press the 'wind back' button to a nasty experience in a past life, then press record instead of play, we could wipe out the original version of events and pop in a new one. The subconscious would not know any different, it doesn't reason or question. It will be happy to remember the new version instead and therefore the ripples caused by the original trauma will no longer be there. And this is exactly what we do in reframing.

To instigate the reframing technique your therapist will ask you to return to the scene at the point just before the incident happened and then choose how you would prefer things to happen. In other words, imagine a more favourable outcome. What you are doing here is recording over the existing version rather like that time when you pressed the record on your little piano keys-style cassette recorder only to discover later that you had inadvertently left your favourite music tape in there and now, right in the middle of the second song, is five minutes of you and your mates playing silly beggars. If you imagine that something different happened, your subconscious will just allow the change. This is done with an intervention from the conscious mind as for just this once you are actually making something up. As this is different to the normal way of proceedings, it has to be done under expert guidance from a qualified therapist, you can't go willy-nilly diving into a past life and tape over your favourite music all over the place, you would create havoc. Once you have been instructed to imagine a favourable outcome, the new bit of 'false memory' then blends seamlessly with the rest of the memories either side of the event. The result? The subconscious remembers differently. It cannot therefore react in a certain way to particular stimuli because it no longer has a reason to. Simple!

One more point about false memory. It is actually a syndrome. False memory syndrome can become a problem if a therapist makes assumptive suggestions to a client's subconscious mind when under hypnosis. This therapy is, and must remain, client led or client based, meaning that the experience must come from the client, coached by nothing more than gentle guidance by the therapist. Certain types of questions must never be asked by the therapist, namely leading questions. Here are a few examples of leading questions:

Are you swimming?
Do you see a building?
I think this must be in Italy, is this correct?

The Many Faces of You

To take the first example about swimming, the client could have said that they found themselves on the beach and the water felt very cold. What they may have been experiencing is the fact that they were barefoot and just walking on the sand at the water's edge. If a suggestion about swimming is made at this point by the therapist the client will start to think about it and then imagine they are swimming. At the instant they do this they've reframed a whole scene, metaphorically taping over their favourite music and now the subconscious believes they are actually swimming. It may take a while to get back on track so it all becomes confusing.

Another useful technique, exclusive to past life work, is to have a meeting with your karmic partners as mentioned before. This is best done at the safe place, the chair in the garden. What you are doing really is communicating with a spiritual being, the soul of your particular karmic adversary. You can invite him or her into the garden and talk about the circumstances under which a karmic imbalance was made. You can tell this other soul how their actions made you feel at the time, how it affected you in other ways and how it is shaping your present day life. In understanding their actions, by asking them to explain their behaviour, you will be able to move forward and reach some form of reconciliation. This will then lead to a very important stage in the healing process, forgiveness. If you are prepared to forgive your karmic counterpart then this will release you from the baggage that you are holding onto, the baggage associated with this particular individual. Once forgiveness has been offered you can perform one or two other actions before sending them on their way. Following forgiveness, there is one more person to forgive, you. Yes, you must also forgive yourself for carrying the burden of karmic debt and in doing this you are enhancing your feeling of liberty. Finally, what about the energy they may have taken from you and held on to over hundreds of years? Now is the time to take it back and, as you are now friends, that should be given back to you freely. Just see it as a cloud of energy leaving your visitor and entering you. There may be cords of attachment here as well, these are like beams of energy which connect people together, acting as the vehicle for countless energy exchanges. The more we interact with any one person the stronger these become and I personally think that these account for such afflictions as 'separation anxiety' when two very close people have to be apart thus stretching their cords. If you have cords of attachment with those that you have interacted with in previous lifetimes, then it causes a permanent link with your own past and this can hold you back in life, especially if the link is a negatively charged one. During therapy you have the opportunity to separate these unwanted cords. The easiest way to do this is have your past life karmic partner visit you at your safe place, the same as before, then visualise the cords between the both of you. They can be seen as beams of light or ropes or any one of a number of options that your subconscious chooses to show you. You are then guided by your therapist to cut the cords in any way you wish. Some will use a pair of scissors, others may wish to hack away with a machete. The important thing you must do is cut it at both ends where it attaches to you and to the point it is attached to your adversary, this takes away the power of the other soul to reconnect. The final step is to symbolically destroy the severed cords and a good old fashioned bonfire is ideal. You are now totally released from any hold that this other individual has had over you.

Another safe place technique you can use is a form of interactive role-playing which has its roots based in a therapy known as Gestalt. You can reverse roles during a dialogue with your karmic counterpart. In other words, become that soul for a few moments, symbolically of course, just so that you can understand their actions. You can ask a question, as yourself and then the answer comes to you when you play the role of the other soul. Have I lost you yet? In the understanding of the other's behaviour you will be able to accept, forgive and move on.

On the subject of meetings at the safe place, there are a few more slightly bizarre interactions you can have in order to bring about healing. There is a Hypnotherapeutic technique called Parts Therapy and this is definitely not one for the do-it-yourself fraternity. This has to be carefully orchestrated by a therapist trained in this sometimes very complex procedure. In a nutshell, we are made up of character parts, Freud called them Ego parts. There is the child, the teenager, the young adult, the parent, the son or daughter plus many more. Each of these parts of our character form at a certain stage in our lives and we call on them in everyday life for the wisdom that they gained when they were dominant. Under hypnosis we can separate out these parts and talk to them as individual entities. The method that I have developed for this procedure takes the form of a meeting in a special building with a table and chairs. You, as the main chairperson, the whole being, sit at the head of the table and can then invite in these other character parts, these can be seen as separate individuals entirely, entering the room and sitting beside you. They will look different in some way, maybe younger, or perhaps a negatively balanced part can look pale and drawn with unkempt hair and clothes. To interact and negotiate for changes, you step into the various visiting parts so that you can be communicated with directly by the therapist.

The Many Faces of You

You take on a different persona and have an understanding of where the imbalances are coming from. You can invite as many parts as required to sort out the conflicts.

We have numerous parts, each one having a different role, but what about all the other parts from your previous lifetimes? Hey, you can call on them as well, let's have a party. Certain parts are dominant at certain stages in our lifetimes, so if something traumatic happens causing an energy imbalance, then that part which is dominant at the time is affected and starts to conflict with the rest of you. Your therapist will act as an impartial mediator to help you resolve the imbalances.

There are many other healing methods that can be utilised in past life work, the more conventional are the standard ones used in hypnotherapy, adapted a little to deal with the more diverse spectrum of encounters experienced in previous lifetimes. As I have said before, some of the healing is automatic and the mere act of experiencing certain incidents will bring about a subtle change of thought processes due to conscious understanding. In other words, "Ah ha, I get it now". Sometimes if you can give some reasoning to a situation on a conscious level, the revelation heals. Couple this with a dislodging of the associated emotion and it becomes all powerful.

Healing means different things for different people. Some will need cures for deep-set fears or emotional imbalances while others just need a fine tune to their thought processes. Reconciliation follows experience and what some therapists do as you exit a past life is ask you to either return to the safe place or rest on a bench just outside the door and reflect on the journey you have just been on. You will be asked to focus just on what has happened and allow a few words of wisdom to spring into your thoughts. These words come from the all-knowing side of you and it is quite profound what some people come up with. It could be anything from, "Now I know why I can't bring myself to hold my sister's baby" to, "I realise now that my relationship had to end like that."

You may be wondering why all this karma doesn't get sorted out on the other side, in spirit. Why don't two souls get together in our spiritual home, shake hands and apologise accordingly. What would be the point of that? If it could happen like that we would soon run out of tests, challenges and experiences. What would be left if we had no karma, would there be any point to life? I think it would be very boring if we didn't have to face our imbalances and tests in the three dimensional world. Surely experience is the whole point of life. Well that's one view, here's another:

The Many Faces of You

It may be all to do with our old friend energy. The karma was created in this dense low vibration world in which we live. If the imbalance caused by the karma resonates at this low frequency then we need a similar situation in which to work so that things will balance. On the higher frequency spirit side of the veil, events of such a low vibration can just not be dealt with.

Past Life Therapy has many other uses and we have hardly scratched the surface. So many everyday ailments have their roots in our previous lifetimes, even the relatively modern ones such as eating disorders. I dealt with a client with anorexia who also had a terrible phobia about eating in front of people. It transpired that in one particular past life she had two separate incidents where food became associated with something bad happening. This happens with phobias, you get two events, the first is called a sensitising event, making the client vulnerable to a reaction and then, if a second similar event happens, this becomes the activating event and off the phobia goes. The trouble with something like food being associated with something bad happening is the fact that we quite often eat and sooner or later something else is bound to happen, thus compounding the problem, feeding the belief. If unresolved in that lifetime, and let's face it, there weren't too many Hypnotherapists in the 19th century, the phobia gets carried forward to the next life. It may lay dormant for the whole of that life and maybe even one or two subsequent ones, but sooner or later an incident will occur and something bad will happen while our subject is doing something with food and then the issues start. In this particular regression my client had a lifetime in Spain in the 1930s and as a four-year-old she experienced a scene where she got lost in the middle of the town of Seville. She was picked up by a woman unknown to her but who was very friendly, and she took the child home. While in a state of anguish she was given an egg on toast. The association was made and she became sensitised to a potential future issue. Years later she ran a farm with her husband and was making bread one day and as she kneaded the dough, she watched her husband working on the tractor from the kitchen window. All of the sudden the tractor moved and toppled over crushing her husband to death. Another association which may have been enough to activate her issues. Time prevented us from seeing if the eating imbalances manifested later in that particular time and she also had another life in between that life and her present one, but something in this life, her present one, triggered this problem. She said she was fine up to the age of 17 and then the eating problems started. Her mind instilled in her a belief that food was associated with something bad happening. To counteract this worry, on some level, she believed the cure to be that she shouldn't associate with food, then nothing bad could happen. Her mind then made the idea of food uncomfortable, thereby causing the anorexia and issues around eating in front of anyone. What then had to be done was a session to deal with these issues on a therapeutic level. The main area that had been addressed was to talk to the part of her that was holding on to the belief that food caused bad things to happen. We orchestrated a meeting with her past life self, the Spanish one who witnessed the tractor accident. During negotiations that part of her was informed about the negative impact that her belief was having on future selves and that there really was no correlation between food and bad things happening, it was just a coincidence that she was making bread when her husband was killed. We also went on to do a little reframing, the four-year-old back in that Spanish life did not get an egg on toast and the adult still had to witness the tractor accident, that's a karmic given, but she was outside and not making bread.

Incidentally, the husband who was crushed by the tractor has reincarnated with her again in this life, taking on the role of a really close and supportive friend.

Emotionally charged past life issues can go back through many lifetimes and therefore must affect all those interim past lives to some degree or another. A client came to see me once with anger problems and this one went all the way back to caveman times. My client, a female in her present life, was of the short, stocky, thick browed Neanderthal type and was angry because the newer, taller and fairer skinned, more intelligent race was attempting to take over their land. In regression she took on the persona of the cave man and felt the strong emotions.

Most past life therapy is there to deal with traumatic experiences which are charged with negativity, but they don't all have to be violent and shocking, although they are probably the most common and they carry emotions of anger, rage, sadness and fear. There are other past life incidents which could carry more complex emotions such as guilt. This is probably one of the strongest and most destructive emotions of all, it doesn't even have an opposite. Guilt whittles away at people and if it is subconscious guilt, as is the case if it originates from previous lifetimes, it can be quite a task to find its roots. Guilt can cause many present life symptoms ranging from phobias to sexual problems. In certain circumstances people's behaviour can be affected and, although a person with the guilt-driven problem knows they are acting irrationally, they are powerless to do anything about it. Let's have a look at an example. Under the Nazi regime in the Second World War, many German soldiers were under orders to eradicate the Jewish race and if they did not follow these orders they would be shot. This sometimes required them to slaughter children. I have done regressions with clients where this has been experienced. How would the soldiers feel, what horrors will they carry inside themselves? The guilt created by having to carry out these appalling atrocities would fester away in their inner mind and then be taken into later lifetimes. Many people alive today would have had their most recent past life in that era, so there are quite a few people going around with really messed up heads. You will find that the people who were involved in these terrible acts will try to vent their guilt and atone for their actions by choosing a career where they are involved in caring for children. This is known as externalisation and they will have many issues about children and their well-being, perhaps being practically affected when hearing about any harm coming to them.

Externalisation manifests in many ways and it is often the case that people take up positions in the medical profession in order to care for others, or they might join the police force to help to protect people.

Sometimes individuals will externalise because they miss what they did in a previous lifetime. There are many who just have to wear a uniform and if they can't join the armed forces or the police, they will involve themselves in the Territorial Army or the Special Constabulary. If you regress these sort of people, you will find that they have had a long run of consecutive past lives in uniform, having been institutionalised so much that they need to reach that familiar and comfortable mindset, standing to attention and being told exactly what to do. Then there are the hobbies and interests. Personally I have always liked the idea of flying an aeroplane although I have never actually done anything about it. Yet I feel I know exactly how to fly, and what the machine would do under my control. This obviously stems back to my First World War lifetime as a German 'flyer' as I referred to it in regression. As a boy I made all the little plastic models of the aircraft of that period, read books and drew numerous pictures of biplanes in dog fights.

Another interesting point about the influence that recent past lives have on us is this, my parents' generation played 'cowboys and indians' when they were young. I played World War I and II soldiers and pilots. Each generation develops its childhood interests based on the era from which they reincarnated.

Past life therapy can take on many forms and each therapist evolves, developing new techniques from the experiences that they have had with clients. What I present here is a fairly generic process so the basics will be the same with whoever you see for therapy. I have then added a few of my own techniques which have been developed over the years. Some practitioners will use a healing technique which is done in the spirit stage following a past life just encountered and I expect there are a few others who will do things that I have never heard of. As long as the end result provides a therapeutic benefit, then that's fine. There are many routes to choose from A to B.

Chapter Four

Returning Home

Lifetimes in the flesh, the ones we visit in regression, could be regarded as excursions. Planet Earth isn't really our home, it's the bit between our lifetimes where we truly dwell and every now and then we choose to have an experience and plan a trip to the third dimensional world. We could choose to go somewhere else and we may not have a physical body on that particular trip, but we always go back to the world of spirit, the other dimension, just behind the veil. I think that maybe the concept of heaven and hell has been over-stylised in the past couple of thousand years and really it refers to the spirit world and here.

However bad we are, however sinful, I am sure we all go back to where we came from regardless of our misdemeanours. Where else could there be? If we reincarnate over and over again which I hope that you believe is the case, then we couldn't be stuck in a burning inferno for eternity could we? Look around at all the negativity, the wars, famine, disease and hatred. No, this is hell.

But we still choose to come here and it is not all gloom and doom is it? It's only negative in places because of our behaviour. Take humans off this beautiful Earth and hey presto, instant paradise. If you love the natural world, as I do, with all its diversity and beauty, then it makes a visit here worthwhile. If you think that the countryside is just mud and the smell of cows then you are missing something great. Having said that, I live in West Devon and it is all mud and cows!

So the spirit world is our natural home, our permanent place of residence and we can reside there without the need of a physical body. No heaviness, no aches and pains, no having to go to the gym. Bliss.

To try to think about how long we have lived in our spiritual home would be an academic folly. We couldn't even start to comprehend such a concept while we are here in our physical bodies, but how long we stay in between incarnations can be quantified more or less when we calculate the dates in regression. It still varies but at least we know. A few years is the average but it can be much longer. What we do when we are back home is also a really interesting question and the best way to find out is to die in one of our previous lifetimes whilst in regression and see where we go.

This is the discipline known as Life Between Lives, or LBL for short. It really is a separate therapy in its own right and some practitioners will specialise in it.

To get to the Life Between Lives period we normally start off in a previous lifetime and go forward to the end of it and experience the passing over. This is nothing to be apprehensive about, as death is just a natural progression to allow the wonderful return to our spiritual home. When you enter the between lives spiritual period your vibration rises and because of this not everyone can have a full experience during their therapy sessions. Practice is the key, as with most things, and people who meditate will be able to have a wonderful journey. I am not suggesting that this is an elitist thing because after a few regressions anyone will be ready, but if someone who has not spiritually developed sees a therapist for the first time they may not do as well to begin with.

The Life Between Lives journey is also very diverse and every one is really quite unique and this is down to many factors, such as spiritual or religious beliefs and expectations. There is a core of uniformity so an experienced therapist will be able to keep track but an open mind is also essential.

All Life Between Lives experiences start off with the feeling of leaving the body, in a very similar process to the documented accounts of near death experiences, known as NDEs where people have technically died after a trauma or during a medical operation. Although of course with NDEs they return to the body and live.

The Many Faces of You

As someone gets the feeling of floating out of their body they can look down and see themselves lying there on their deathbed, in a crumpled car or on the battlefield, wherever they die. They can also hear any conversations that go on around their body. The next thing that occurs, in the majority of cases, is the feeling of being drawn upwards and entering a tunnel and, again, this manifests itself in several ways. The pull along this tunnel becomes very strong and at the end of it there is a beautiful and powerful light of some sort. This is spiritual energy and the feeling in this light is one of love. As an individual experiences this feeling during their regression they go very quiet and unresponsive to the therapist, feeling totally in awe of the sensations. Eventually communication starts again and information is relayed.

From this point the journey can take on various forms. Some of those newly arrived home will be met by a spiritual being, sometimes it is someone they know, a family member that has passed over before. In other cases it can be an angel or some other form of light being. For others the journey may take them into breathtaking landscapes more beautiful than anything on the physical Earth, incredible vivid colours and exquisite plants and views that can hardly be described. At some point everyone will be met by someone or something and guided to the next stage.

Time has little meaning in the world of spirit so I really cannot explain how long each phase of the journey takes. Some say it feels like it is all happening at once, others will see the experience in well structured stages.

At some stage, after some rest and reintegration to settle our newly-raised vibrations, an appraisal of the lifetime just departed from has to be made. Again this can take many forms and this is where the religious idea of judgement comes from. The important thing to know is that we only and always judge ourselves, there is no angry God pointing the finger. No one has an opinion and there is no punishment for any erroneous deeds that we have done during the lifetime now being appraised. This phase is often called the life review and it is really mind-boggling for us mere mortals still here in the flesh. Every action, every moment and every thought is projected in front of the viewer all simultaneously. The way you made someone feel when you argued with them can be perceived, the way you felt when someone did you wrong, every aspect of the life being reviewed can be experienced. Quite often during this review we are helped by others and there are usually three of them. This has been referred to as the judgement board but that really is an inappropriate name because they are not there to adjudicate, but to offer assistance and guidance as we reconcile ourselves with the consequences of our actions.

The Many Faces of You

When you originally planned the life that you have just left you chose your aims and goals and in some cases there may have been just one major lesson to learn. The life review allows you to compare that original blueprint with what actually happened, thus giving you an understanding of what could or should have been done. Your life may have gone according to plan in which case the lesson is learnt and there is no need to give it to yourself again. Members of the judgement board may assist as you evaluate the lifetime under review, offering guidance and direction with regard to future lives and tests.

Following the life review there are a number of things a soul may choose to do. Some will get on with the task of planning for the next incarnation, others might decide to stay at home for a while to rest and contemplate.

There are schools of learning in the spirit world and they have been described as temples in one form or another, huge elaborate structures with pillars in the ancient Roman style. This may be an interpretation, of course, put into a form that our LBL clients can comprehend. I am sure that in their true form, energy, they are very different. Newly-arrived spirits may choose to enrol at these places in order to help them gain the knowledge they need to progress to higher levels.

There is one question which is bound to be asked and it is to do with the location of our spiritual home. The trouble is that we can only think in three dimensions as this is what we see, we can only think in linear time, because this is what we experience in life, so to get further than the concept that heaven is just behind the moon we find it difficult. Let's think multi-dimensionally and use the analogy of a radio. Each station is on a different wavelength frequency. Only the station we have tuned in to can be heard, all the others seem to just not exist. However, every station is there in the atmosphere all around us all of the time and because we have radios designed to detect certain frequencies, which are basically vibrations, we can grab hold of these frequencies, but only the ones our box of tricks has been designed to recognise. There are a massive number of wavelengths out there, some for walkie talkies, others for TV sets or mobile phones, yet another one again for our computer's WiFi or cordless mouse. The point about this analogy is the fact that all these frequencies are in existence all around us yet we are not aware of them unless we have a suitable detector to show us that they are there. The spirit world is probably like this too, a whole other world in the same physical space as us but vibrating at such a high frequency that science has not been able to make a device to detect it yet. It would have to be something very sophisticated and interestingly, they do actually exist. Yes, the device that some people have for tuning into the frequency of the spirit world is called a Psychic Medium, also referred to as a sensitive or just someone with the gift. The mind-blowing sophisticated complexity of the living soul makes things that we have invented, like the radio, seem like a stone being thrown compared to a modern missile-seeking laser beam. A psychic can tune into the spirit world so easily because it is all around us, the only reason we cannot see it is because we are unable to perceive anything that has a different frequency to ourselves. We can't see radio waves can we?

In the spirit world there appears to be a number of levels of frequency which go up in steps and it is understood that as we evolve ourselves we can ascend to the next level. Even in this better place it is still all down to rank and hierarchy. Again, any ideas about what these higher levels are to do with or feel like must be subject to a fair amount of speculation as it is far beyond our normal logical thinking. When you reach level seven, which some people assume to be the top, then I guess we have achieved the ultimate goal and I can't help wondering what happens then. Some say you reunite with the Godhead, the source, that which we are part of. So the seventh heaven is our final destination but let's not be in too much of a hurry to get to it, the journey is just as good. Does a mountain climber enjoy the climb more than the standing on the top? Of course, otherwise he would just hire a helicopter to plonk him onto the summit. I am making this sound like some sort of anti-climax but I'm sure it is not and I shouldn't think that spirits in the lower levels of evolution even know what the top level, the penthouse, feels like. You are not stuck at any particular level either because higher level beings can still move about in the lower levels or even reincarnate if they wish. I was once told I had reached level five and yet I've been an insurance salesman in this life, how the mighty have fallen! All these higher stages are probably where the more evolved souls dwell, such as Angels and then perhaps the big boys, the Archangels are further up. And what about Jesus? There are enough people outside Christianity who believe he existed. I am not convinced personally, but I think a generic character portrayed as Jesus is representative of any number of level sevens who have popped down to see us through the ages in order to give us a bit of focus.

When we die, or rather when our bodies malfunction sufficiently to prevent occupation by a soul, we detach completely and there is no going back. However there are other ways to leave the body and retain the ability to return. The Near Death Experience is one such example and some of the documented cases have suggested that an individual can take quite a journey into the spirit world before being dragged back. Some will go through the tunnel, meet loved ones and even get presented with a part of their life plan. They sometimes get told that this is not their time and they must return to their body. It seems that if the body is fully alive and can sustain life then the soul has little choice in the matter and must occupy it. There are many people who, having experienced this phenomenon, expressed dismay in having to come back. It must be jolly nice over there.

Another way to experience out of body experiences is to go Astral Travelling and this can be achieved by people who have advanced themselves spiritually through meditation and other activities. A connection with the body is maintained by a silver cord which is like a very long spiritual umbilical cord. Astral Travelling is basically flying about the place in full consciousness away from the physical body.

Remote Viewing is a form of Astral Travel where your awareness can float above the body and can go anywhere in the world and see what is happening. This can be achieved by most people while being regressed and it is a very useful way to help a person to find a missing soul fragment stuck somewhere in a physical location on another part of the planet. Its saves a lot of time and money too as the alternative is to lug your body there to find it via road, rail or air.

I think we also sometimes unconsciously leave our bodies when we sleep as well. Sometimes as we start to drift off to sleep we suddenly do a sort of jump which wakes us up again. Some people believe that this is caused by the soul leaving or returning to the body. You may even go off into one of those other dimensions where we are leading a completely different life. The reason I say this is because some dreams are so different and contain such highly detailed architecture and landscape that our subconscious couldn't possibly be producing these by using references from information stored in its archiving. These can't be past life dreams either because they are set in modern times yet the scenes experienced seem very real, detailed and three dimensional.

So the bit when we are not inside the present body is very complicated. The marvellous vehicle that we use, constructed of the elements that grow around us will eventually go wrong and release us. Our journey home is also varied and appears in some part to be adjusted to our present life beliefs and understandings, probably to help us with the shock of dying. A devout sceptic who thinks that you die, and that's it, would not cope if his or her soul were immediately met by angels and taken to their life review. So, they may just be given some quiet basic place to rest until they adjust and start to remember. A Tibetan monk may be presented with something that his lifelong faith can identify with until he's ready to move on, it may be different from how he imagined it to be. A Christian will be totally confused if the first thing they hear is talk of reincarnation. The spirit world must be vast, complex and multifaceted to be able to create a unique temporary reality for every individual that passes over.

As the newly-arrived begin to integrate, their vibration starts to rise, becoming in tune with their surroundings. As this happens the knowledge they had before reincarnation slowly returns and it will start to make perfect sense. In some cases this can take a long time, maybe years and some spirits go into a sort of rest period like a long hibernation, especially if they have just left a very hard life. So our knowledge returns but nobody really knows what this knowledge is, of course, because we are here in the flesh, thus having forgotten. We can certainly glean some of it in our Life Between Lives journey and this will teach us something about ourselves, our purpose and our own personal journey. By having this experience we become privy to this special wisdom and this can help us to think differently and reach our full potential in life. Gaining this higher knowledge about yourself, your sole purpose, is called 'spiritual integration'. You know your path.

Going back to the passing over journey once more, many Life Between Lives clients have periods of quiet during their journey as they are so in awe of their experience. They are in another place and feel far removed from the therapist's couch. The main thing that stops them in their tracks is the beautiful light at the end of the tunnel, it is described as an all-encompassing brilliant light which carries with it a wonderful sense of unconditional love. The client will have a taste of how fantastic this feels, consequently temporarily abandoning the therapist. Here's a tip, if you would like to have a Life Between Lives therapy session, find a patient past life practitioner!

Out of this light the next step develops and more often than not you are met by someone and guided somewhere. The soul who meets you may well turn out to be someone who was close to you in the lifetime you have just left. As you are still adjusting to the higher frequencies your total knowledge would not have returned yet so it would be no good being greeted by the soul who was your mother in the life before last, you wouldn't recognise her. Therefore those in spirit form must have the ability to present themselves in a guise which can be recognised. This can't be their normal appearance, they are spirit after all, your granny in this life may have been your brother a couple of lifetimes ago so they can't look like everyone they have been. Initially there must be a feeling of being totally lost so it is reassuring when you are met and guided by someone you know.

The Many Faces of You

As I have already stated, the life review usually follows this initial stage but again there are many variations. Instead of a large panoramic presentation others will see a book, their book. This is a complete record of their whole existence and they can turn to the pages which have the record of the lifetime just left and the life review is made. In some regressions clients do not even encounter their life review and this is to do with the higher frequencies of the spiritual energy, they become less visual and work more with feelings. In one Life Between Lives case that I have worked with the client felt very aware of their own feelings and sensations, especially of their heart. This client stated that she felt totally centred around her heart because that is where the consciousness is, not the brain. This must be true to a point because heart transplant patients have been known to take on the memories of their donor.

At some later stage in the proceedings the soul prepares for reincarnation and this is sometimes done with a little reluctance, it is like leaving a cosy warm log fire to go out into a blizzard. Planning a lifetime is a complex and meticulous task taking into account numerous factors. For a start you have to choose your parents and they have to provide you with the required set of lifestyle circumstances in order for you to fulfil your life plan. Each life you organise will have specific tasks to do to provide the necessary experiences; these may be to do with some karmic imbalance which you need to sort out. This karma could be with a place or a person so the geographic location of the parents will have to be considered and that is of course the easy bit. When it comes to sorting out all the crossing of paths with your karmic partners throughout your lifespan, and these partners also having to do the same thing with their life plans in order to synchronise, then the ripple effect of all these chance encounters and interactions would take more than the world's most powerful computer to work out. When you think about it doesn't religion simplify things? Why is it that a devout follower does not consider such concepts even if their chosen faith embraces reincarnation.

I guess the planning of the next life would have to involve hundreds if not thousands of other souls to get the whole interactive network to work. No wonder it all goes pear-shaped when we are back here in this low vibration, it is probably a hard job for our Higher Selves to direct us.

Our return to the flesh is now imminent. We have arrived back in the spirit world, become re-acclimatised to a real environment, had a really good look at our behaviour in the life we have just left, perhaps had some learning, planned our next life and now this is it. The transition from spirit to bodily occupation is not always experienced by the clients undergoing Life Between Lives therapy as they just see themselves floating above their new mother then bang, they're back. Occasionally though there is a more detailed account of this magical transition. If you think about it you have probably got to retrain yourself to occupy a big lump of meat because once you are in it autopilot kicks in and you have no control.

Here is an extract from a Life Between Lives case. The client came to see me with a specific desire to experience the between lives state. This describes the way our spirit bodies prepare for our solid bodies. I will put my interjections in italics.

*   *   *   *   *   *

I see a field and it is harvest time.

Tell me about yourself.

I am wearing a blouse with flowers on it and a sort of pinafore with buttons down the front. A full skirt down to my ankles. My name is Harriet and I am 40 years old.

There are men cutting hay and we are gathering it up, carrying it in our arms and laying it in some sort of pyramid shape and then you start another. The men are cutting the hay with the scythes and the women are picking it up. I lean against one of the pyramids.

Tell me how you feel at this point

Just reasonably happy, peaceful, it is quite hard work but I don't mind.

Now I want you to move forward in time to the last day of your life here as Harriet. Allow your mind to take you to the final day of your life, your life as Harriet.

I am sitting in a chair in a cottage feeling very sleepy. I am now 70 years old.

How does your physical body feel?

Like it is slowing down, just worn out. I feel happy and have had a hard life.

It is now time to experience your death, your death as Harriet. Move forward until this time and tell me what happens next.

I still feel like I have everything about me ... I still have and feel the aura ... I can see me now in the chair and I am moving away.

I know I've left.

How does it feel to be free of your body?

Light ... gossamer ... misty ... airy fairy ... moving very fast now ... but the awareness of 'me' has gone. I feel I have crashed through something ... like the edge of an orb ... a sphere ... like going through an egg shell. It snapped shut behind me ... I physically felt it at the back of my head. I am floating now ... not aware of any shape to me. I now feel jostled ... other entities like me there ... it's calmed down.

I feel very aware of my heart now ... as if I am my heart. My heart and brain seem to have merged.

What does this signify?

That the mind is in the heart ... not the brain.

Please move on to the next step of this journey.

There is a golden light ... nothing else ... I am seeing with feeling rather than with eyes.

How does this feel?

Doesn't particularly feel that lovely ... it just is.

What is the purpose of the golden light?

Acclimatisation ... the shedding of vibrations. I feel heavier ... I was rising but now I feel heavier ... like a settling ... like a lying down to sleep.

Please move on to the next stage.

I am in a sort of room ... I have an awareness ... a domed room ... very high. It is still golden but white at the top. I am aware of my heart again ... seem to be giving my heart. I've joined ... I don't know what ... to become one. In my physical body I want to cry tears of joy ... euphoria ... there is a feeling of gratitude ... grateful in heart.

What do you do here?

The domed room is a last vestige of a physical imagination ... and now I'm just in the oneness ... there is just nothing.

Thank you ... please now move on to the next stage.

Gathering something around me ... very aware of sensations ... arms and hands ... seem to be gathering awareness. I am holding a sphere. I am now aware of descending.

Tell me about the sphere.

I'm still puzzled ... it is now gone from my hand and I only have a memory of what it felt like. Misty. Feels like a faint breath after a long time of not breathing. I just feel I need to get a breath into my lungs.

Tell me how you feel both physically and emotionally.

I do not feel much aware mentally, my brain seems to be blank. I am aware of my heart again ... must have lungs ... needed to practice ... training. I need to learn to breathe.

Look around you now and tell me what you see.

I can see the Earth now ... the sky ... the stars. I become aware of my stomach ... and then the legs ... feeling the back of my head. My system is becoming physical ... teeth ... bones ... getting stronger ... arms and face.

What can you actually see at this time?

Only aware of sensations ... darkness. I'm all there and I'm going to be a girl. I feel where my breasts will grow. I feel a turning ... a sensation of turning ... being born ... I think.

And what can you see around you now?

Nurses ... scales ... busy. I have cramp in my right foot. Very aware of nerves and a sensation of touch ... auto nervous system ... shaking ... very nervously aware.

My name is Beth and it seems like 1943.

*   *   *   *   *   *

This was a different version of events from the norm but who can really say what the norm is? The existence in the spirit realm is so complex that we can just not experience it all in regression; it could be because it may take a very long time. It would seem that during regression our Higher Self chooses only certain extracts for us to view, based on what we need to learn at this time. The part which actually helps us in life is the planning of it and of course this is only useful if you have just regressed to the Life Between Lives state which occurs just before your present life. If you find yourself dying in Elizabethan England, then an understanding of what you planned to do in the lifetime that followed may not be much use. It will help you to understand some karmic patterns but those particular set of circumstances may not be of relevance now. You could have already solved that karma a couple of hundred years ago.

The Many Faces of You

I would say that a good proportion of Life Between Lives clients cannot experience the next life planning stage and there could be a good reason for this. This knowledge has been held back from our Lower Selves because if we knew everything we were meant to do then conscious intervention and free will would interfere and really mess things up. There is nothing like a cocky consciousness to think it knows best when clearly it doesn't.

If you are reading this book as a qualified Past Life Therapist and would like to find out more about Life Between Lives work the experts to refer to are the Newton Institute. They are well known for this particular therapy offering quality residential courses all over the world. For further reading on the subject the books by their founder Michael Newton are recommended.

Free will is an interesting topic. This is our wild card or maybe our get out clause. Whatever our life plan has in store for us we can still choose not to stick to it and on some unconscious level we know what's what and yet we can still take control and alter the outcome. Life in the third dimension will offer many flaws which can prevent certain things from happening. Everything that happens is not predestined and the smallest aberration can have a devastating effect on our plan. For instance, gravity could completely kill your whole complex synchronicity-based path. To give an example, supposing you were soon to go off to work and you decided to make some sandwiches as you knew you would be out on the road somewhere. What if you accidentally let half a teaspoon of mayonnaise drop to the floor unnoticed? This is where we blame gravity because the next thing that happens is that you slip on this spillage and crack your head on the fridge door which you have not yet closed. Down you go in a haze of stars landing in an awkward heap on the floor. Gravity again you see, what a rascal. You feel so groggy that you suspect concussion and abandon work and go to the doctor's instead. Now, if you had gone to work that day you would have met the person that you should have met and eventually fallen in love with and then marry. Tell me, was it in your life plan to slip on that spilt drop of mayo or was it just one of those random events that happen? Either way this chance experience has changed everything and what about the person you should have seen that day? It's made a right old mess of their life plan too and all the other people they should have interacted with. One drop of salad dressing and that swine gravity was all it took to cause mayhem in the life plans of hundreds of people.

Still, the universe is very clever and when something like this happens, and let's face it something like this always does happen, it starts a very clever recalculation, a bit like a sat nav in your car when you ignore it or miss a turning. It plans another route. The idea is to get you back on track however long it takes. Perhaps in our scenario, your appointments are rescheduled and you finally get to bump into your future betrothed.

But not always.

If your planned path is this messed up you may not get back on track at all. Whether it is that little bit of mayonnaise or your own free will to choose to ignore what should be, your projected plan may suffer irrevocable damage. No wonder we keep having to reincarnate, we just have to try and get it right next time. Once you are out of balance with what you should be doing you are in freefall and everything in your life might go wrong. Work will suffer, finances may as well. If you miss the chance to meet the person you should have met then you may meet someone else and it just wouldn't be right. You could feel lost and out of control. Now is the time to listen to the universe, act on your feelings and take notice of chance meetings with everyone you cross paths with. Somewhere there will be a message from one of these people which will help guide you back on track. Remember that there is no such thing as coincidence, everything is there for a reason so listen and analyse the conversations you have. Jump in the river and let the current take you. No, that was a metaphor; we don't really want to drown!

The use of free will is not always complete folly, sometimes you may have a choice in life and your free will may improve things, giving you a different experience but still one of great value. There is no right or wrong in life and all we can take back with us is love and knowledge so any occurrence is good for us whether positive or negative. Life is about tests which we either pass or fail. If you get it right then you may not have to face that test again. If you get it wrong then you will have to build that test in to a future life.

I am fond of the onion skin analogy. These tests in life are like layers of an onion, each one bigger than the last. If you are successful in a task set before you then you peel off a layer of the onion. You may well get the same challenge in a later life but it will be a smaller one if you are successful the previous time, a smaller onion skin. Again if you get that one right and peel off another layer of the onion then any subsequent similar tests will be milder. On the other side of the coin failure will result in a layer being added, a bigger onion skin. This means that next time the same test will be harsher, more of a challenge. It is all linked in with karma, as many of the tests we set ourselves are to do with an imbalance and will normally involve other souls. When we finally really learn the lesson and clear the karma we are then at the centre of the onion and therefore have exonerated ourselves, wisdom has been gained and the lesson learned. We won't get that test again. I would guess that if you have a major challenge to deal with, a very large onion layer, then this will play a large part in your proposed life plan. A small test, one which has been successfully completed in previous lifetimes may just be built in as an aside.

As you experience regression to your previous lifetimes you may well notice these onion skin patterns emerging. To get the full picture you will need a few sessions visiting many different past lives, but it pays dividends because you will recognise that test in your present life and know how to deal with it. A keen subconscious will show you all the lifetimes which carry this particular challenge, but only if it is appropriate and important in your present lifetime. In other words if you have planned to have this particular test in your present lifetime, then your subconscious will help you prepare. This viewing of connected lifetimes is called Interlinking and if your inner mind is really enthusiastic you will find yourself seemingly randomly jumping from one lifetime to another in an uncontrolled and confusing fashion. A good therapist will recognise what is happening here and guide your subconscious to show only one past life at a time.

Chapter Five

Into The Future

This is where it all gets very interesting. Not only can we regress back to our former lives, we can also go the other way and look at our future ones. Although this will be presented in great detail one thing I will not do is tell you how to access your future. This is definitely not one for trying out for yourself; you will need a suitably qualified therapist.

To understand why it is possible to view something that hasn't happened yet we need to understand one very important concept. It's that thing we never seem to have enough of, there appears to be less of it when we get older and it never seems to be available when money is.

Time.

We understand time from a three dimensional viewpoint, a linear sequence of events. It marches forward in one direction and is measurable. Outside the limitations of our solid world time is more fluid, more malleable; it sort of overlaps itself and what we see as past, present and future meld together in the other dimensions. To try to demonstrate what I mean here is an analogy.

If you were in a small canoe paddling along a river in a deep ravine you would only be able to see as far as the first bend in either direction. This is a representation of how we see time in our physical world, not being able to experience anything but the now. If you could fly above the narrow valley you would still see the little canoe but you would also see the whole river in its entirety, every bend and every series of rapids. This is a representation of time in the spirit world, a much bigger picture. By observing the topography below you would know exactly what will happen to the canoe and see what has already happened.

The present isn't actually all there is, it is just that bit in the middle sandwiched between the past and the future. It is however the most important part of time for us while we are here on planet Earth. It is the culmination of everything we have done and it is the blueprint for everything we will do. Really we should relish the present more. Look at the world, it is the best present you could ask for. We waste the present worrying about what we have already done in the past and we also waste it worrying about what will happen in the future.

Tomorrow's future will be our present when we get there and our current present will be our past. Did we waste it worrying? The important thing here, and the reason I am wittering on so much, is this:

Whatever we have done in the past, whether we have worried about it or not, it has created our present. If we had done something different back then, so our present would have changed. It follows, therefore, that whatever we do now will shape our future and if we decide to do something different today, our future will have a changed outcome. Think of all the futures we could end up with depending upon what we do right now.

Here's the twist. All of those alternative futures can be explored in hypnosis. It is almost as if the future is just a scenario based on our present behaviour. The exact things you do today will create a fixed future. If you change your behaviour today, make new decisions or change direction then your future becomes not only fixed again but often quite different.

This is what journeys into the future are all about, creating a favourable future life by modifying our behaviour today.

Time therefore is fluid and flexible and, given that, you could say that every future scenario has happened already. Are we then back into infinite dimensions, every scenario of our lives being acted out by a different facet of ourselves? I bet you would love me to come up with the answers wouldn't you? Sorry…

The therapy that can take you forward in time is called Future Life Progression and in some ways the experience is similar to Past Life Regression, it is the reason for doing it that differs. There are two distinct areas within Future Life Progression, your future lifetimes and the future within your present life. The latter will be discussed later. A visit to your future lives can be really fascinating and it will show you how the world is shaped in years to come and how your part is played within it. Probably the most popular future life to have a look at is that which follows our present life. Personally, as a therapist, I am always very cautious here as our subsequent future life can present clues about our lifespan in this present lifetime. This is not a good thing really as I believe that it is fundamentally crucial that no one has an inkling when they will die. To quote an example, let's suppose a therapist was conducting a Future Life Progression session for a 21 year old and the next lifetime was only 20 years into the future. What does that indicate to the client? That he or she will die before they are forty. One has to be careful and only visit the next life on rare occasions and with older clients. Either that, or instruct that their subconscious does not have any concept of dates.

As you can already see, Future Life Progression does have moral ramifications and each case must be appraised and treated carefully. Once we go beyond the next adjacent future life, perhaps a couple of hundred years or so then all is plain sailing and some very special experiences can be gained. This really is the stuff of science fiction as we race around the future in our virtual time machine. This does not mean that the future is rosy of course, the chances are that things may well get worse before they get better but we have to accept what will be, because as individuals we can't change the world.

But we can change ourselves.

This is the main point of Future Life Progression. The knowledge of our future can help us make it how we want it. Because time is fluid, our future lifetimes will be fashioned out of our current behaviours. It is this multi-dimensional thing again. If we progress into our very next sequential lifetime, what we see is what will happen given our current circumstances. If we choose to change our present conditions and behave in another way then a subsequent Future Life Progression session will produce a different future life.

The future is a scenario based on our current behaviour.

The Many Faces of You

If therefore, you don't like the look of your next lifetime, change what you do now. Of course some, or probably most, of your life reconstructing will be minimal and your new future life scenario may be similar with perhaps just a few subtle differences. This is a bit like the modern way of mending a car; you keep replacing parts until it goes. To fine tune your future you have to keep changing bits of your life until you attain the required outcome. Other factors may affect your future lives as well, such as your other previous lifetimes. All the behaviours that have gone before shape your present life and the future ones too.

You may find yourself asking what the point is. Why worry about your next life when it's hard enough to run this one? Good point, perhaps there isn't any point at all but before you throw the baby out with the bath water consider this, if your future life is happy and karma free, then whatever you have done in your present life to make this happen must be beneficial. Your reward for your present actions is shown in your future.

What will you find when you travel off to a lifetime in another few hundred years? If it will depend mainly on what life you choose and where you plan to have it. If you put yourself in a city the advances in technology are very evident and we see hovering cars and intelligent homes with sophisticated computers built into the structure.

There are unusual advances in energy use, thank goodness, and I think the oil barons will finally fall. There seems to be little evidence of spiritual advancement and, as 2012 has been and gone and the world didn't end, we can look forward to what happens next. Fashion changes constantly but we don't appear to all end up wearing space- age silver jump suits again, thank goodness. In some progressions into the near future, say 50 or 60 years, all is not so well with our wonderful planet as pollution is much more evident and the atmosphere appears smoggy. It looks like we need to get our act together and find a way to take away the power from the oil industry so that all the other carbon-neutral technologies can break free from their present suppression.

The good news is that the world does get better and the further we go into the future the more positive becomes the energy, and the cleaner the air. These future scenarios are more fixed compared to our individual projections as they are governed by the collective consciousness of the human race. We can modify our own behaviour to create a different future for ourselves, but the environment we find ourselves in will be more or less the same. Only a huge shift in the way we all think as a species will change that.

A popular topic within Past Life Regression is soul mates. With whom have we shared our past lives, and why do we have so much affinity with some people, yet have an instant dislike for others as soon as we meet them? If you have a real bond with someone you will probably be able to discover many shared past lives. It is the same with the future too, we will meet again. One client I saw had tragically lost his wife at a young age. He had grieved and was now seeking answers. Why did she have to die, where is she now? He really just wanted a personal spiritual experience first-hand to confirm the existence of an afterlife. It was a difficult regression in some ways as his subconscious seemed to be blocking access to past lives. He was a good subject and visualised well but every time he tried to explore a past life shared with his wife it all went blank. When this happens I usually have a chat directly with the client's subconscious mind to see what its agenda is. It is quite often the case that people are seeking answers, but they don't really know what answers they want as they don't really know what the questions are. The subconscious does though; it knows exactly why they are there. So I ask it. The answer for this client was that he wanted to know about his late wife, has he had lives with her before and will he have lives with her again. I thought that the best person to answer this would be his wife and in this unique space, under hypnosis between our world and the next we can do just that. I had him invite her into the garden at the safe place, that nice place where the comfortable garden chair sits. He visualised her arrival very easily and felt her presence then asked her why she had left him and will they share other lives together. She confirmed that they would definitely be reunited and also agreed to accompany him into a Future Life Progression to show him a future shared life. She waited while he entered the future life and as he explored he found her, again as his partner. After he was satisfied he came back out of the door and his wife accompanied him back to the garden where they said their goodbyes and she left. This was a very therapeutic exercise for my client providing closure and optimism.

People who undergo Future Life Progression often find certain personal traits emerging just as they do in previous lifetimes, not only behavioural aspects but also vocational and occupational ones as well. These common threads run right the way through. If an individual found themselves in ancient Egypt designing those architecturally beautiful temples and perhaps in their present life they are a motor mechanic, you may find that these completely different skills will combine in a future life and they may be involved in some sort of research and development of a new type of transport or fuel. We learn these skills in each lifetime for a purpose, they are not wasted when we die. So here's a thought, why not explore your future and bring back the ideas and knowledge of all that advanced technology and use it today? You can be sure it's not that simple, if you really think about it. In that future life you will probably have spent most of your adult life developing a project and you will hardly be going to grasp it in a twenty minute Future Life Progression. Besides if you did use the technology now you change your future anyway so you would not be doing what you saw yourself doing in your future. It gets a bit complex doesn't it!

Before you grab your mouse and look for a Future Life Progression therapist on the internet ask yourself one very important question: Do I really want to see into the future? I suspect that most people will say yes without a moment's hesitation, but consider the downside of all this knowledge. What if you explored a future where you found the world on its knees, choked with pollution, all the rainforests finally chopped down, seas risen so much with the melting ice caps that a good portion of the land is now under water. You may feel the negativity, how despondent would that make you? I'm not saying that this will be the case, some futures look very rosy indeed and that depends on the physical location of your chosen future. A green, recycling, zero carbon footprint vegan would be badly affected by such a vision and they could even change their way of thinking. What is the point in what I'm doing, it changes nothing?

On the plus side wouldn't it be wonderful to know if all those scaremongers were right or wrong, all the doom merchants who want us to be environmental and economical with our water to save the planet. They obviously don't live in West Devon, it rains all the time here! A detailed Future Life Progression would surely prove one way or the other, mainly to yourself course, that global warming is just a political exercise or that crop circles really are made by the Earth's rising vibrational frequency. You can go into a Future Life Progression with specific questions and ask your subconscious to show you the answers. Fascinating!

Now we know the secret of Nostradamus, as all he did was a Future Life Progression or two. His actual name was Michel de Nostredame a Frenchman who lived in the 1500s. He wrote down many future predictions, in a form of poem or sonnet known as a quatrain, a four line prose, and they were very cryptic. He derived his future forecasts using a form of divination known as scrying where he looked into a bowl of water and really focused. Sounds like hypnosis to me. Some of his predictions were frighteningly accurate, while others were way off the mark and I think the reason that some have not come to fruition is all to do with the idea that predicted outcomes are just scenarios based on present circumstances. A lot can happen during the centuries between his forecasts and the time when they were due to happen. Who knows, they may all have happened in other parallel universes. Free will coupled with the collective consciousness of the human race has shaped our world now, his future then. Yes, this guy was doing Future Life Progression back then.

Pre-cognitive dreams are another form of future exploration. Occasionally someone will dream of some sort of global disaster long before it happens. Some get documented and go into the public eye but most will probably get dismissed as coincidence. One has to question why it is only the devastation-type events that get dreamt about. It is probably not the case but perhaps nice ones get ignored and I think that our spirit guides, or something in the Universe, give us a nudge when we are in the dream state, in contact with our subconscious/Higher Self, so that we can do something about it. As most of this chapter suggests, the future is not set in stone so certain things can change and disasters be avoided. If that's what they want of course, a follower of conspiracy theories may well point out that some disasters were planned and may be unavoidable.

A journey into the future is quite straightforward with a focused mind, and at any time when you are focused and less aware of your surroundings you are in a form of light hypnosis. When a gifted tarot reader looks at their cards they connect with them on a very deep level, synchronising with the different energies that each card projects out. Once in the zone they can easily predict future outcomes. Here is the complicated bit, and if you are a card reader and totally disagree with me and feel I don't know what I'm talking about then maybe you're right. When someone sees a tarot reader they shuffle the cards, which on the surface is something that would appear to be totally random. What if their Higher Self has an input and on some marvellous spiritual level could feel the different vibrations of all 74 cards and put them into the correct order before handing them over to the reader. At this point the cards hold the energy and order of the client so when the reader spreads the cards out and deeply focuses on them, and goes into hypnosis, perhaps they can then act as a psychic surrogate and go on a Future Life Progression on the client's behalf. This idea could spill over to any form of future readings and predictions, including astrology.

The gift of future knowledge is there for the taking, the only question is what to do with that knowledge.

This brings us on to the other side of Future Life Progression. Your future in your present life. I am not alone in having reservations about this part of future exploration and I refused to embrace it for many years. It eventually dawned on me that with a few simple safeguards this can be very a helpful technique.

The reason for exploring your future within your present life is to help you with current decisions and choices. If you arrive at a crossroads in your life with major choices to make, it would be really beneficial to see where those choices will lead you. Two or more outcomes based on your focus and questions as you begin your Future Life Progression can be explored. To illustrate this let's have a look at an example:

You are in a work situation and someone has approached you with an attempt to headhunt you, offering a very attractive package with more money, a company car and other fringe benefits. In your present position you are doing very well and promotion is on the cards. You know your present job very well and feel very comfortable where you are. The new offer is very attractive with a bigger and stronger company, a better package but tinged with the unknown. You spend days in dilemma trying to decide what to do, stay put and feel safe and confident or take the gamble for a better opportunity and lifestyle. A Future Life Progression would give you the chance to see where each choice would take you, the alternative paths.

With 'this life' Future Life Progression I only feel comfortable in projecting forward two or three years and this would be fine for the example above. The most important thing to consider here is a client's mortality. If you had a client project twenty years into the future and they discover that they become ill or have even died early, and perhaps that part of their future may be set in stone as part of their fixed life plan, then this knowledge could change them. It may even bring on the illness through the anxiety caused by the knowledge. Yes, this insight may provide an opportunity to change their lifestyle in order to prevent this happening, but the future they have been shown will be there as part of their conscious memory, creating long-term worry. When conducting a 'this life' progression I am always very vigilant in making sure clients are blocked from seeing the limits of their lifespan. They will be totally prohibited from seeing their future demise.

There is a slightly darker side of future exploration in your present life. Some therapists will entertain a future exploration for personal financial gain. "Bring it on", you may say, and yes it does sound like a good plan. The trouble starts when it steers you away from your own personal life plan, what you should be doing. You will find that the Universe is not all that tolerant of personal indulgence and will block certain activities so it's no use having a look for next week's lottery numbers, you are just as likely to be steered into some sort of corner by universal intervention and be shown the wrong numbers. The purpose for our existence is to do what we planned to do, so if we are destined to win a fortune then perhaps one in fourteen million Future Life Progressions will show the right numbers. I will expect you to say "So what, it's worth a shot" and I don't blame you. If it is part of your life plan to see a therapist for Future Life Progression then this stepping stone in your life is right for you.

Future Life Progression has been utilised to show an employer how a prospective new recruit may get on in the company and this is a good example to demonstrate the whole point about future work: scenarios. To have a future life experience to observe a potential new employee the client must put him or herself in the mindset of having decided to employ the applicant, so really this is simply a useful guidance tool.

Some elements of our future may be fixed, other parts will have differences dependent on our free will choices. As individuals our future scenarios can be quite diverse but they are usually still played out on the same stage set out in the bigger picture, the planet's future. In so many years certain things will happen here on our planet regardless of our individual actions. In the melting pot of the Earth's population's collective behaviour, a true and fixed set of circumstances are bound to emerge. If you look back over time you will see that we are, as a race, fairly predictable, not one faction of ideas and beliefs becoming dominant over the rest. True, many have tried to achieve a global shift in human thought such as the great dictators like Hitler but it all just keeps simmering away, man's evolution keeping to the plan. It follows therefore that any exploration into the far future will show similar results from one individual to another. And wouldn't a glimpse into our world thousands of years from now be really interesting? One thing that is very apparent is our ineptness at being able to imagine what our future will be like, you've only got to see a 1950s science fiction film depicting the future to see how wrong they were. Showing a scene set in the year 2010 way into the future all clad in silver jumpsuits talking to a home computer as it cooks the evening meal, a silver tube of a vehicle hovering in the garage. No, I think we evolve at a much more sedate pace than we imagine we will. Here is a progression into the far future to illustrate the point.

I asked my client Joanne to project herself into a life a very long way into the future and the year she first settled on was 3012. This was a very interesting life as it was actually on a different planet, my subject being one of another more evolved race altogether. Interesting though this was it gave us no reference for our quest to discover the evolutional progress of our Earth- born successors.

The Many Faces of You

I then asked Joanne to find a lifetime here on Earth in the far future and she found a lifetime to explore in the year 5000. The account below has only been altered to make smoother reading, no factual details have been manipulated.

*   *   *   *   *   *

"I can't see much, it's all just sand. Oh, I can see me now in a robe, full length and knotted in the middle. I am wearing a turban. I am a 76-year-old male but my body feels fit and well. I've had parts replaced, it's not the body I had at the beginning. Every time a bit wears out, it's replaced."

I asked her whether these parts are purely mechanical or made of flesh, she said both. She continued:

"I can go back now, I needed to leave. Back to the town. I see white coloured buildings, towers, some big some small, near a river that still flows but we have to clean it to keep it fresh. The climate has high temperatures some storms, sand storms."

As the names of geographical areas change over time I felt it would be folly to ask where this was so I did a little exercise to find out where in the world she found herself. This involved a little remote viewing and I had my client imagining lifting out of her future body and raising high above the Earth, then looking down and seeing where in the world she was. This is what she told me.

"You would know this place as Damascus but it is not called that now."

I then returned her to the ground and asked about her role in this future life.

"Some sort of records, we compile records, collecting information and dates. This information is stored on microchip. The room in which I work is light, a big square room. There are other workers around the edges. The floor looks ancient with a beautiful mosaic. We replace it when it gets broken, we don't have to have broken things."

I then asked her to go about her business.

"We have to retrieve the knowledge and collate it, we have to know everything. I cannot explain where this knowledge comes from but we keep it safe for our own ends. Knowledge is power, we have to know everything."

I wanted to know why they are so protective of this knowledge, who they were keeping it from.

"The others, those that would rule us from all directions, we have to keep it safe. We hide the knowledge from them."

I then asked her to move to a domestic scene as I was intrigued as to how they lived.

"We all have our dwellings and we live as large, extended domestic groups, not necessarily all related. Our dwelling is light and airy, thick walls, mosaic floors, cool inside, we do not go outside very much. There are separate quarters going off, smaller groups. We are always on the alert, always ready to defend our knowledge"

I finally asked her about any forms of transport she was aware of, as I am interested in future technology.

"We do have transport but we don't use it often. We can get into the shuttles but don't need to. If we do it is usually to get supplies."

*   *   *   *   *   *

It would seem that we haven't all evolved into limbless slugs with huge brains and having robots that do everything for us, which is good news. In fact, this example does seem to demonstrate much less evolution than we would expect in another three thousand years. Some elements show technological advances such as human longevity by the use of replacement parts, yet buildings seem very similar to what we have now, as do the clothes. We still appear to squabble with other cultural groups so there is no change there. The fact that they are processing electronically stored knowledge would suggest to me that this is discovered information, much of it being new to them. For me the lack of evolution in terms of dwellings and costumes along with the learning of this knowledge would suggest some sort of post-apocalyptic world where we may have had to start again. When you look at advances in technology in the last hundred years one would expect an awful lot more in the next three thousand!

Let's see what else we can discover about ourselves as we journey from one lifetime to another. They say that there are as many stars in the sky as there are grains of sand on the beaches, a concept hard to imagine. How many of these bright burning suns have planets spinning around them? If there is only one in a billion that's still an awful lot of planets, quite a few beaches worth of sand. Of those how many are inhabitable? It could be an incomprehensible number, would you be able to count the grains in a handful of sand? The common denominator here is the fact that all these suns, planets and moons are part of the physical world, the third dimension, the one we presently occupy. Well most of us anyway, as I expect there is some help with this book from other realms, for which I give thanks in abundance. It follows therefore that we need not be restricted to having lives here on planet Earth, we are not just Earthly souls, we are Universal souls. It would also be a fair guess to say that we don't always have to experience different aspects of life in physical bodies but we quite often do. I mentioned earlier the first of Joanne's two Future Life Progressions, the first one being set on another planet. This just happened to be one of her future lives but could just as easily been one in her past. As far as evolution goes I suggest that the beings that choose to occupy the Earth are, when here in the physical dimension, really quite primitive and I am sure that there are races out there whose evolutionary advancement would make us appear as not much different to the amoebas we share our big round rock with.

Joanne's Case study set in the year 3012:

*   *   *   *   *   *

The access into this lifetime isn't a door as such, more of a space with bright yellow changing lights, moving lights.

"I am wearing robes but nothing on my feet, the clothes are very light, creamy white with bits of blue. I can only describe my physical body as floaty.

I'm in the city and there is movement, people and vehicles like oval capsules that open and you just climb in.

As for my purpose, I tend plants and herbs. Medicine, growing for medicine. These are housed in a big dome, we have to make the water for the plants. The plants are large, bright colours and we use the pods, all different types. Some of the plants we have made ourselves as we can't get them anymore. We all have our jobs to do and we are told what to do. There is no free will anymore. It is the people in central government who tell us what to do, we are watched.

To communicate with each other, some sign as there are a lot who cannot hear, they put all the deaf people down here. I cannot hear, I point. I can see but can't hear, I don't need to, we just know. We get our instructions through the vibration of sound and thought. I'm in my own dwelling place now and there are a lot of us eating at regimented lines of tables. We eat small coloured things, nutrition. There are different sections, can't sit with the others. The young are set aside, we don't need to see them. I only see workers and controllers, I don't have a family. Emotionally that is just acceptance, a sort of numbness.

The Many Faces of You

The world in which we live has a name that sounds like Niquar, it is in the seventh solar section. I have no knowledge of the history and evolution of our species. I'm now in the centre dome, we are all here. There is a new governor coming, the old one has gone. There is extra security today, we can't move freely. He's coming now, escorted, it's not going to be good. It's not good but we can't do anything about it, we have to accept. At least what we do is safe."

*   *   *   *   *   *

This alien life depicts a complete lack of freedom and the workers seemed to be little more than drones. There always seems to be a hierarchy where a few control the many, even in alien civilisations. This begs the question, is life on Earth really all that bad?

We now see that the future is a scenario based on present actions, those actions in turn shaped by our past and there is another very simple technique to help us with our future choices. I developed this particular procedure to help clients who have a difficult choice in front of them and I suppose it can be regarded as the light version of a full blown Future Life Progression. It is called the Future Choice Meditation and it starts from the safe place, which is the chair or something similar where a client under hypnosis rests following a descent down some stairs or steps. The choices the individual has are discussed prior to the hypnotic induction and normally there are just two choices to consider but more can be added if the therapist is good at multi-tasking, so if you are a male therapist you should stick to just the two. Once the client has been instructed to leave the safe place they are guided onto a pathway which is normally a fairly wide clear one through a forestry. This leads to a T junction where they see a signpost. On this signpost there is a single word written for each direction, representing the two choices the client has to make. The words are usually suggested by the therapist and as an example one direction could be 'move', the other 'stay'. As long as the explorer understands clearly which path represents which choice then all is well. This is called a meditation rather than a progression because not only is it guided and led by the therapist, which is unconventional in this field, but the ongoing journey and exploration is also symbolic rather than factual. The journey then explores each direction, first one way then back to the signpost at the T junction then the other way. Each of the two experiences will be different, quite often the symbolic imagery showing negative elements in one direction, positive ones in the other. This experience usually makes it abundantly clear which is the best way to go so they can then make up their mind and get on with their lives. To reiterate, this is not an accurate glimpse into alternative futures, it is more like a symbolic guidance helped along by the spirit world. Like all symbolic imagery it can be modified to suit an individual's circumstances so if you have lots of alternatives to consider your therapist can always construct a roundabout!

You can try this future choice meditation for yourself and there is a script in chapter 8.

The future is yours to explore. You can choose how your future will be, to some extent anyway. Perhaps it is right to say you can choose how you run your own life in your future, but the environment in which you find yourself is beyond your control, it is more or less fixed and you have very little influence over it.

You can have a glimpse into next year to see how your latest project is going, you can quickly have a look at next week to see it you get to your next Future Life Progression appointment.

Or you can choose not to know.

Chapter Six

Journeys Into Far Pre-History

We have seen how things could work out in the far future but these are variables, all conjecture. With our past it has all happened and is unchangeable and what we observe in our past life journeys is what has happened, so this is a complete and accurate record of everything that we have experienced until now.

Going beyond the usual three or four hundred years, the normal date range for average Past Life Regressions, it all gets very interesting. We are not talking about a few thousand years here, more like many millions. A journey into far pre-history will bring you a very wide range of baffling experiences, which in some cases are so bizarre you couldn't make them up if you tried.

We haven't always been the beings that we are today. Our souls have remained the same, perhaps just more evolved through learning but our bodies have altered considerably. The universe, God, call it what you will, may have created everything but once it was all wound up, set down and let go, it evolved. Darwin gets a brownie point or two as well. If you research all the fossil remains of our predecessors you will see that we have not always had the shape and form that we have today, that being Homo Erectus, Upright Man. Evolutionists will show us a gradual succession of species from monkey to man presenting this as an evolutionary journey. When they find the missing link then I may consider accepting what they say, as I am sure there is an input, some divine intervention if you like, from the universe to help boost our development from time to time. We needed a body capable of housing our spiritual self and also it had to be very versatile and dexterous in order for us to express our intelligence. Without some help it would have been an awfully long wait for Mother Nature's seemingly random selection programme to finally fashion a suitable flesh-built vehicle for us to inhabit.

What did we do before our modern bodies were ready for us? Occupied whatever was available? I personally have never been a follower of the idea that we reincarnate as animals but through research into far pre-history I must concede that we certainly have been animals in the past. I still don't believe we would come back on all fours these days, I think we have evolved too much for that. There were many millions of years before man came along, looking like a man. And where are all the souls of the dinosaurs now? Here is a case study that may just answer that question.

Sally came to see me as a volunteer to help me with my research into far pre-history. She was very good at regression and had an incredibly interesting result:

*   *   *   *   *   *

"The door to this lifetime is like skin, I just touch it with my foot. My body feels quite small with funny little legs, and a long tongue like a lizard. I have thin legs, four of them and the front ones are small. I am light brown in colour and I have scales. I'm in a clearing within the trees, big plants everywhere. There are others which look the same as me, another two or three. We communicate by making a loud screeching noise. We move very fast, have to. We keep a constant watch, have to be safe. We can run swiftly and hide, we go into holes.

We have come across a huge egg and we break it to feed, you have to be quick. We get surprised, we run fast, run very fast off in different directions so predators can only get one of us. There is an angry giant with big teeth, we run. We wait until it is safe and then we move on."

*   *   *   *   *   *

So there you have it. We were here long before our human bodies were. It may help to answer a question: What happens to the souls when the animal they portray on Earth becomes extinct? It's like going to the train station but there are no trains and there never will be. So what do you do? Find an alternative, a taxi or a bus. So if all those animal souls can't be Sabre Tooth Tigers anymore perhaps they might volunteer for Lion duty instead.

The case study about dinosaurs is very interesting but this is about far pre-history and quite honestly a mere 65 million years into the past just doesn't cut it. For me pre-history goes back in time so much further, long before we were occupying any comprehensible bodies.

And then of course there is the argument about the population of other planets. The Earth is still an incredibly young chunk of rock compared to others and there must have been a time at the very beginning when it was totally uninhabitable. But we still existed and we weren't made especially to live here I'm sure. So when we explore further back in time we won't always home in on an Earth-bound life . However, we do appear to be present on Earth in times so ancient that they defy the scientific consensus about life. It would seem that we were here to generally step over the primeval soup from which it is assumed we evolved.

I have two examples of completely separate cases of very early times conducted years and miles apart from each other yet they have a remarkable number of similarities. The first one is with Sheila.

Sheila actually came for therapy and hoped that Past Life Regression would help. She was suffering from anxiety and frustration and an exploration of a couple of past lives showed us nothing new, the same feelings were present there as well. On my instruction to go way back to the original cause of these symptoms she started to go back in time very quickly, almost flying down the path and then she eventually slowed down. This is her account and as with most of the case studies presented in this book it has been modified just enough to keep it interesting, leaving out my questioning. All factual information is retained.

*   *   *   *   *   *

"All the doors down at this end are of a different shape and look modern. They seem to be made of some sort of shiny metal like stainless steel. To open them you just push a button. I am through the door now and looking down at myself. I am sort of web toed, my legs are more like frogs' legs jointed. but not at the knee. and they bend forwards. I wear no clothes. I have very strange skin like a very thin translucent leather, no pattern on the skin and the colour is a browny beige. I'm possibly slightly taller, but not much.

This is a fairly barren land, flat with red soil and I can see for miles. I am not told where this place is so I don't know. We don't live anywhere specific, just live where we happen to be. We get messages that tell us where we have to travel to. To travel from one location to another we are packed. We all sit in a long rectangular container with seats on either side, it flies. Everyone else is exactly the same as me. When we arrive at our destination the container opens at one end and we walk out. On the outside the transport looks like it is made of stainless with ridges down each side, running length wise. All sides look identical and there are no windows.

We travel to these different places because we are told to go, we get messages which we see inside our mind. The messages also show us pictures of what has to be constructed. It is like a 3-D picture, we all get the same picture at the same time. There are between one and two hundred of us here. I am a worker, like an ant with no thoughts of my own. My body is sophisticated though because I can move from one place to another by just thinking it. I think this is how we aid the construction of what we are developing, with thought."

*   *   *   *   *   *

We left it at this point because I felt that we still had more work to do with regard to the anxiety-related symptoms that she sought help with. I asked her subconscious directly where we should go next and what would be even further back than that.

Sheila did experience something else and we will look at that later but first I want to present another pre-history regression which had similar details to Sheila's.

Emma came for a general curiosity-based Past Life Regression and was very nonplussed by the dull lifetimes she had explored. She was very good at regression and I could see that she wanted something more, so I suggested a journey into far pre-history and she jumped at the chance. Here is her story:

*   *   *   *   *   *

"The entrance to this life is like a portal, a vibrating round thing with different colours and bright lights. To go through, I just think it. I am wearing transparent white flowing robes and I have a large head, large eyes but no hair. I'm just floating and to move I just think it.

There are mountains, craters and caves around me and also the city which I see in front of me now. It has tall thin transparent towers and there are halls and side places for the workers. The walls and pillars are like crystal, glass. In the room I am in now there are three chairs and this is where we get our instructions and guidance. Those who give us the instructions are known as The Three and they are here now, they materialise if I think them here, if I need to see them. They give me my next task. I am an overseer.

My next task is to do with research. The young, we have to have perfection, no faults. I am a scientist and I work in a laboratory and there are cases where the young grow, they grow from a program and we have to take the faults out. The young have big heads and small see-through bodies, mostly they are heads with large brains in various stages of growth. I make sure everyone is doing their job, they all have a task. We create the light we need by thought.

I am somewhere else now, with the workers. These are ugly things, but useful to us. They have less brains than me and they are larger than us. They have a wide face and mouth, small eyes and they are physically stronger. They mine for us bringing the crystals we need for most things, for power. We are not indigenous to this planet, we are far and wide, we move. We are superior to the workers, we brought them here to work. They are supplied, transported in capsules. These capsules are a vessel for transporting, we have others. Those which supply the workers you would compare to a cattle truck, these are airborne trucks, powered by crystals. Inside is a control area which goes around the edges and the workers are in another section behind. You move fast, we have people for the task, assigned."

*   *   *   *   *   *

Although many of the details in the two regressions differ, there is an overall common thread with the idea of drone-like workers being crammed into a metal box and taken to the next project. There are also similarities in the way that these things from ancient times communicate, through telepathy and their method of movement, through thought. I cannot tell from these two examples if the beings portrayed were indigenous to our own planet or if indeed it was Earth they were visiting.

There is quite a lot of evidence from other sources which would suggest that our world has been host to races that are far superior to ourselves. Some may have been visiting aliens who chose to stay, others could have perhaps been evolved from animals of which the remains have never been and probably never will be discovered. This is all such a phenomenally long time ago where empires could have risen and fallen, returned to dust due to certain cataclysmic events, only to start again on the evolutionary path.

The importance of crystals is prominent in Emma's regression and this is also regarded as the main source of power in the well-documented ancient land known as Atlantis. Many psychically sensitive individuals have tuned in to the vibration of this wonderful bygone forgotten era of Earth's history and I have also regressed one or two clients back to that time. Some believe that many of the souls who incarnated at the time of Atlantis are now returning to Earth to help with her evolution, raising vibrations and helping others on their path. They are referred to as Star Children and Light Workers.

Atlantis was in existence for eons and went through a number of evolutionary changes, unfortunately for the worse. It is not really clear how it all fits in time-wise with all the other pre-history events experienced through regression but I personally think it was fairly near the beginning of mother Earth's occupation. The reason I think this is to do with the disposition of the early Atlanteans in what has been referred to as the Golden Age, the earliest era. The first Atlanteans had a much lighter body than the ones we have now and by that I don't mean they were size zero waifs. The make up of their bodies was less dense, more like a heavy gas than flesh. Again it is all to do with vibration, the higher the frequency the further apart the particles of matter and, because of this much higher frequency, some believe that they could step in and out of the spirit world as their vibrations were so similar. Of course, once they started to experience more and more Earthly pleasures their vibration lowered and their bodies became denser and their ability to travel inter-dimensionally then diminished. In other words, the more negative things became the lower the vibrations and the heavier the material became.

The Atlanteans also had a wonderful knowledge of the power of crystals and developed ways to harness that power. There is even a belief that they had crystal-powered flying machines like balloons with propellers, other accounts suggest boat-shaped craft that could land on water. As the planet's vibrations started to fall and greed, materialism and the hunger for power increased within Atlantis it all started to go wrong, eventually ending in a huge cataclysmic event caused by the loss of control of a great power crystal, causing Atlantis to sink into the sea. Some people believe that following this disaster the survivors travelled all around the globe and it is interesting to observe that there is a common thread to a race that includes the far eastern occupants, such as the Chinese, the Mongolians in northern Russia, the Inuits in Alaska, right down to the indigenous people of South America, all with a similar appearance. Could these be the descendants of the original race on Earth, the Atlanteans?

Everything presented so far is just a little further back than yesterday compared with the true beginning and the second of Sheila's far pre-history regressions really did go back to the year dot. I asked Sheila to find the time just before her very first incarnation into a physical body. Make of this what you wish.

*   *   *   *   *   *

"There is fear, sadness, hopelessness, complete despair, myself and thousands of other souls have been caught, trapped. We didn't know that evil existed. The shock is almost too much to bear. Before this happened there was total peace, happiness, surrounded in love and beauty. I cannot find the words to describe how perfect it can be. We have been in this perfect state of Utopia forever.

A light suddenly appears, even brighter than the light in which we exist. We find ourselves drifting towards it then we are unable to return, we are all ensnared and we can't get out. We are trapped in a nothingness, invisible barriers holding us there. We are all in shock, completely numbed, we are prevented from being within the energies we have always exchanged, shared. We can now only exist as a small part of what we have been, like a small flickering flame just managing to survive. This period lasts hundreds maybe thousands of years, complete misery.

We are shown a way to move forward, given a choice to either stay as we are for eternity or to inhabit bodies of flesh and then to act as slaves for our captors. To be born into a body gives a feeling of suffocation, absolute repulsion. It feels so, so wrong. I feel I can never forgive myself for doing it. It is almost as if I am in alliance with evil giving myself over to escape this misery. It feels like the body is manufactured ready for me to inhabit, but I am not sure, as I can't see it. I am no longer in control of what happens. Everything is so difficult, it will take a long, long time to adjust. Have to learn to do everything, never had a body before.

I do not see my captors, but I feel them. This is a new game to them giving them something to do as they are bored. They build places to control us from but they don't need to live in places themselves because they are still forms of energy.

This makes me feel like we have always been caught here, right from that time and only through hard work and understanding and evolution can we escape this treadmill."

*   *   *   *   *   *

I will leave it up to you to decide what this all meant.

And then there are the Egyptians. I often wonder how accurate the archaeologists are with their account of when this advanced race was actually living here on Earth. They say just a few thousand years ago, yet many among the spiritual community reckon the pyramids were built much earlier at around 10,500 BC. I think it could be further back still but who really knows. There is a huge amount written about ancient Egypt but much less about the time before the Pharaohs ruled. How did they evolve into such a powerful and advanced race, building huge and architecturally perfect structures while the rest of us were living in mud huts? Are they from this planet? Where are they now? You would think that modern Egypt should reflect its past in a different way to what we see. I have performed many regressions to ancient Egypt and they are all fascinating, depicting such things as architects who designed and built the ancient Temple of Thebes, to servants and slaves. One of the really interesting ones involved my client as an ordinary person in the street who worked for the Pharaohs, in quite a good position but was certainly not one of the nobles. One day he awoke to find that every single member of the royal family, and their inner circle - the lot with the sloping foreheads and the fancy headgear - had completely disappeared, vanished off the face of the Earth never to return. The same thing happened to the Mayans in South America, all disappeared without a trace. Did they ascend into another dimension or wander off in their spaceship to wherever they came from? One day I hope to have the answer.

Whilst on the subject of aliens, they also get involved in pre-history in a malevolent way. We hear stories about certain people who seem to be repeatedly abducted and regression studies reveal that they are experimented on and have their reproductive organs harvested for breeding programmes. There is a good reason for this regular kidnapping and it is to do with some sort of bizarre contract that certain individuals have been scammed into. This contract is known as a promise and to hold that agreement, something is inserted into them, a bit like a beacon, so that they can be found in the future for further abduction. These implants are not necessarily physical, more like a lump of energy and they can be removed by spiritual healers sometimes. These contracts were quite often made a very long time ago and it is as if these souls are owned by the aliens. Over many lifetimes the pattern of regular abduction takes place. I had a client once who was scared of death because she knew they would be waiting for her at the edge of the tunnel once she had left her body. She would have to run the gauntlet to make it to the light.

Whether you accept that there are aliens or not is another thing and the idea of them actually being able to land here in the first place takes some believing. The nearest planet could be so far away that it would take at least a lifetime travelling at the speed of light to get here. Perhaps we have to think outside the box and consider an idea that is believed by many that these other worldly beings come from other dimensions, the fourth one to be precise. To be honest I'm not really sure what the fourth dimension is and I don't think anyone else has the right to think they know either, but the idea that aliens travel from other dimensions and just materialise once in our atmosphere is quite appealing. Spiritual healers also deal with entity attachments which include malevolent alien beings hiding in our auras, further strengthening the idea that they are inter-dimensional.

The reason that aliens are featuring in a chapter about pre-history is to do with the fact that they are not a modern phenomenon. Throughout the millennia it would appear that they have been visiting and many very ancient cultures depict unusual looking beings in space suits in their artwork.

I once conducted a very interesting alien abduction session with a client who was exploring a past lifetime in a very ancient culture. She didn't experience the normal surgical procedures that you hear about but these beings did behave in some peculiar ways. In some way they harvested energy from people taking it from their very soul and then they stored it behind some sort of force field barrier located on the far side of the universe. We had to do some serious astral travelling to get it back. This case is certainly peculiar but isn't anything remarkable when it comes to the extraordinary and the unexplained. The fact that so many sightings and abductions have been documented without one decent photo or piece of video footage would suggest that anything is possible. Let's not forget that we have probably had previous lifetimes as aliens. Once on the other side we are just part of the pool of souls waiting to reoccupy the third dimension, which let's face it, is pretty big! Lots of planets to try out.

Chapter Seven

The Weird and the Wonderful

If you think you have read some pretty weird stuff in this book so far you haven't seen anything yet!

The inner mind is a mysterious wonder, its flexibility and accommodation always surpassing our wildest expectations. Just when it has all started to make sense I plan to stir it up with a presentation of the more unusual techniques that can be employed by the advanced Past Life Therapist.

Let's start off with a simple one, the third party observer. Occasionally when someone is being regressed they stand back and take on the role of the onlooker, watching themselves in a past life from some vantage point or other. They may still relay their experience as if they were actually feeling everything that is going on, speaking in the first person or, on the other hand, they may give a running commentary from the viewpoint of the third person. In some cases they may even be above the scene offering information from their bird's eye view. There are a number of reasons why this happens, the main one being protection. They feel safe if they are just watching an event rather than being a part of it, another reason is the inability to go the whole hog and observe from inside their past life body. This is an involuntary action controlled by the subconscious for reasons beyond our understanding. Occasionally a therapist may instruct a past life traveller to step out of their past life body to relieve any of the slight physical discomfort which could very rarely be felt by the client while regressing.

Now here's a question. If you are in a Past Life Regression and find yourself standing behind your former self observing what you are doing, then are you, as the third person, your present self? And if this is the case how can you as your present self be in the same past life as your previous self all at the same time? Could you even talk to your past life self? Well, yes you can and we will look at that a little later on when the plot thickens. Another question which arises from this funny little scenario is this, when you were that past life person in that scene in that previous lifetime on that particular day at that precise time, did you feel a presence behind you as if you were being watched? As with many stories about time travel does your mere presence as your present self in your own past life, watching yourself causing this feeling of being watched, influence your past life self in that scene to a point that a different outcome ensued? If so, and I'm only just getting started so hang on, is who you are today fashioned by a disturbance caused by your future self in one of your past lives? There, hands up who wants to read that last bit again.

Time is fluid, life is inter-dimensional and if both statements are true then the above scenario could happen. To put all this into a bit of perspective, we can't actually change anything that we haven't changed already. This is where Past Life Regression parts company with the science fiction version of time travel. If we affect something by visiting a past life, especially if we are there as a third party, it doesn't mean that when we come out of regression the cat has become a dog and you find you have married your childhood sweetheart instead of the lady whom you have known and loved for the past 20 years. This is because anything you affect in a previous lifetime has that effect there and then, it is already part of history and your position in the universe today is because of this effect which happened a long time ago. To put it another way, if you weren't destined to have a regression in this lifetime which would have affected the previous lifetime then the butterfly effect would not have happened and you will not be a different person and therefore would not have married your childhood sweetheart, all because back in 1497 you weren't visited by your future self from 2013. Time for a nice pot of tea I think, don't you?

The Many Faces of You

I stated earlier that you can visit a previous lifetime in a regression and actually communicate with your past life self. Whether this is a totally symbolic meeting conjured up by the subconscious with the help and guidance of your therapist, or this actually happens, with your past life self being visited by an aberration of its future self it is hard to say, but it can be done and the only important thing to consider is, why do it? Well there is a point to having a conversation with your former self and it is to do with the therapeutic side of Past Life Regression. There may be an issue, the original cause of which came from a past life that has an effect on your life today. The part of your character that made you the person you were in that particular previous lifetime could be causing an imbalance with the rest of you and therefore needs healing and rebalancing. By talking with your former incarnation you can bring into your present-day consciousness an understanding of your behaviour back then. You can observe your actions as they are played out and here's the odd bit, change them. Yes, if you don't like what you did back in 1842 you can go and tell yourself that it is wrong and inappropriate so don't do it.

Now, I would expect a few of you to be questioning my integrity as a Past Life Therapist having presented you with the above. I wouldn't blame anyone for wanting to reject these more extreme aberrations but before you do perhaps we should just take a few steps back and consider what is happening here. Let's have a fresh look at the subconscious mind and the way it functions. The whole concept of Past Life Regression is the fact that we are we reliving memories and these memories are fixed, set in stone. Remember how the subconscious records and stores these memories, as data archived away in chronological order. These memories are preserved in much the same way as you would record a television programme on a tape, DVD or hard drive. Once it has been given information to store its only function is to provide that data in the form of knowledge and wisdom, never to be analysed, questioned or lost. Our subconscious mind has no ability or interest in any part of what has been archived away, as far as it's concerned it is just information. To flog the TV programme analogy nearly to its demise, regression is when we press rewind taking us back to a previous lifetime, and we experience it in our mind's eye when we press play. Moving to a later period of that lifetime is when we press fast forward. If we can do all that, and we can because the subconscious functions in the same way as the video recorder, what happens when you press record? Well you should know the answer because we have discussed this already. We change it. By visiting yourself in one of your past lives and encouraging yourself to do things differently you are effectively adding a patch of false memory onto your tape or DVD. The subconscious then has a different memory filed away. When it scans that event for any references suitable to provide wisdom for similar experiences it just reads the newly modified record and acts accordingly. Therapeutically if a past action creates a disturbing imbalance in your present life then changing the memory removes the emotionally charged issue. This technique is a recognised hypnotherapy procedure known as "Reframing" and it has already been covered in its more conventional guise in the chapter on therapy. It has been reiterated here to demonstrate the bizarre permutations available for the Past Life Therapists trained in such advanced procedures.

Now we know we can visit our past life selves, as always, we can explore further aberrations of this. Not only can we go into a past life as our present self and talk with our past life self, we can also invite one of our past life selves to meet us at the safe place, the chair in the garden or wherever. And the reason? I hear you ask, well it saves us the bother of going down the pathway to see them, all we have to do is bask in sunshine and ask them to come to us. The same negotiations can take place, a two-way conversation to help you understand the mind of your past life character's behaviour. And while you are there you can also invite along other past life selves from different lifetimes and have a party. Well no, not a party, in reality this is a complex therapy and the idea of a meeting with a number of past life selves is to balance and harmonise the parts of you which are so unbalanced that they are affecting the other parts. Of course you have to be aware of your previous lifetimes where your guests have come from and furthermore you must be made aware of the imbalance between them all, so this sort of therapy can only be undertaken once a number of sessions have been done. I think a little story will help to explain.

*   *   *   *   *   *

Tom went to see a Past Life Therapist with a huge hang up when it came to attractive women with red hair. He really adored these titian beauties, they were his type and he would choose one over a blonde or brunette any time. He was a bit of a playboy, a Jack the lad and has had many relationships over the years. He had come to see the therapist to try to sort out a most unusual and awkward problem. For some inexplicable reason, he suffered from anxiety attacks if he was with a red-haired girl and she wanted to drink red wine. White wine was fine as was any other drink. If he was dating a blonde or a brunette then if she drank red wine there was no problem but a redhead with red wine brought him out in sweats and he became a quivering wreck, begging her to have something else to drink. He was regressed to the cause of this fear, his subconscious indicating that this stemmed from a past life back in the early 1800s. He found himself in a love triangle and he was madly in love with the lady of the mansion where he worked as the butler. Her husband was a monstrous tyrant and she grew to hate him, finding solace and love in her clandestine relationship with her manservant who was Tom in this previous incarnation. They hatched a plot. They would do away with her husband and she would play the grieving widow, living alone and being looked after by her faithful butler, or so it would appear to the rest of the world. The chosen medium to dispatch her husband would be the poison arsenic, dispensed by the butler into the man's glass of red wine at a dinner party. There would be many guests that night, their presence compounding the number of likely suspects, should foul play be suspected. Annabel sat with her husband at the head of the table, her features framed by her locks of fiery red wavy hair. The butler personally chose to serve the wine that evening, carefully decanting the toxin into the husband's glass. With the wine served the butler withdrew, casting a quick knowing glance at Annabel. Soon they would be together.

And then it happened, disaster struck. Annabel suddenly choked, went pale and slumped onto the table. The whole room erupted into a kinetic frenzy and a doctor was called but by the time he got to the house Annabel, his beloved, lay still and cold. Later that evening the evil husband accosted the butler and said "I've known what's been going on for ages and I've switched the drinks on many occasions in anticipation of what happened here tonight. I'm glad she's dead and I will make sure that you swing for this."

Four weeks later the butler was reunited with Annabel as his soul left his twitching body on the end of a rope.

*   *   *   *   *   *

Tom's soul returned to spirit in trauma, wracked with the guilt of killing the woman he adored, the repressed emotion further compounded by his execution. This entire imbalance was then carried to his next life, an easy one to plan as both he and the soul of Annabel were in a position to plan together a new life where they could meet again and enjoy the love which was so cruelly taken away from them. Well that was the theory anyway. To make sure they were in a close relationship they decided to reincarnate as brother and sister. They would go into their new bodies a year apart, Tom's soul first and then his new little sister would follow. All was well when they were both tiny but as they grew a little older the boy started to behave strangely towards his red-haired sibling, becoming overly protective. The problem grew worse as time went by and one day when he was seven he went berserk when he saw his mother giving his sister a glass of blackcurrant drink and he flew across the room knocking the drink out of her hand shouting "no!" The problem grew worse over the years and his behaviour heavily tarnished their relationship.

Many more lifetimes followed and Tom carried on these issues from one life to another always attracted to flame-haired women and always acting strangely should he see them drinking dark red liquid.

This little story demonstrates how an individual's action in their previous life can have a domino effect on subsequent incarnations and this produces a number of unhappy, ill-balanced past life selves. A meeting with these dysfunctional past life character parts would help to bring about reconciliation and a new balance. Such a meeting could be held in the garden or in a special building with a table and chairs, our present life regressor would chair the meeting and under guidance from his therapist would negotiate with these other aspects of himself, perhaps convincing the butler that the blame should be transferred to Annabel's husband and forgiveness should be offered. The other past life selves can then gain understanding of the behaviours they exhibited in their particular lifetimes which would in turn lead to acceptance and finally putting the imbalances to rest. Other healing techniques can also be employed at this point to fully balance and harmonise all the affected parts of our subject's character. Our present day Tom would eventually find that he was free from the anxiety he used to feel when in the company of redheads when they are drinking red wine.

We can go on yet another step further in the realms of past life interactions. You must remember that many of the more unusual scenarios shown here have been developed by Hypnotherapy South West so you will not encounter them with Past Life Therapists who have not trained with me.

Another interactive technique of mine has the unglamorous title Consulting Your Past Life Healer. This entails a visit to two different lifetimes, but as your present day self. Certain criteria have to be met before this process can happen. First of all you need to establish if you have had a past life as a healer of some sort, a Hedge Witch or Shaman perhaps. Then there needs to be a different past life where you suffer from an illness. If by chance you encounter both these elements during your regression you are then able to set up some powerful healing. As you experience the previous lifetime where you were ill you become aware of the nature of the illness, how it feels and the possible connotations with regard to the feasibility of recovery. We must bear in mind that back in the days before modern drugs, fatalities from relatively minor illnesses were high. You then leave that life and journey to an earlier incarnation as a healer, usually an earlier one but it can be the one after the life when you are ill but let's not complicate things any more than they already are. You visit your past life healer in the third person, meaning that you remain as your present day self from your current lifetime and actually meet the earlier self who has the role of the healer.

A consultation about your other unwell self is conducted and the healer is asked to supply you with an infusion of herbs and perhaps other ingredients that will treat the symptoms that your ill self is suffering. Then, remaining as your present third party self you thank the healer and return to the other life where you have experienced the illness.

You can now either administer the remedy to the patient yourself or ask another carer, if present, to do so for you. After that has been done you can either observe the recovery from your third party perspective or elect to become the unwell past life self again, so that you can feel the effects of the medicine. Not only are you healing that lifetime on some level or another, you are also bringing some of your earlier wisdom about healing into conscious awareness.

There are some elements to these strange advanced techniques which fall outside the boundaries of rational explanation and the inquisitive mind will want all the "i's" dotted and the "t's" crossed. On what sort of spiritual or energy level does this occur? Did that Hedge Witch actually experience the meeting with the stranger they felt they knew? In their delirious state did that person who had been the patient see someone unknown to them arrive with the perfect solution to make them better? Did they actually physically receive that herbal remedy or was it a vision, a moment of clarity when they knew exactly what was required and told their carer who then blended and administered the ingredients. It doesn't really matter, as the important thing is that it made a difference which had a positive effect on the client in their present life when they came to see their therapist.

Here is a case study demonstrating the Consulting Your Past Life Healer therapy, but like many things in this book there is a twist because Pat, the client here, was not the healer in a previous lifetime, her daughter in that past life was and is now her best friend in her present lifetime. Pat came to me for ordinary hypnotherapy to deal with her fear of vomiting which she had developed over the past five years. We did some conventional regression techniques in order to find the childhood causes and there were certainly issues already there.

However we could not find a cause.

* * * * * *

I asked her to regress using the doors in order to keep an open mind on whether this was a present or past life issue. As she looked for a door she went beyond her present lifetime into the past and found a Georgian panelled door representing the early 1900s. She was wearing the attire of a service maid with a crude linen apron. Her name was Elizabeth and she was in her early teens.

She found herself in the hallway of a grand home with large Georgian sash windows.

I moved her forward in time to a significant event which connected with her fear.

"I am close to crying, a child, my child. There is a bed. I am a woman in bed giving birth. Now I feel myself standing at the foot of the bed."

We had to finish there and on her return for her next session I asked her to return to this lifetime a few days before the time she found herself in bed. I asked her to describe how her body felt.

"Heavy, I don't want to go into the body. Feeling ill now, sick, scared and heavy."

I asked if her body was unwell or was it more to do with the fear.

"It is a physical illness. I am wearing a dark gown and I am in that hallway again feeling very tired. I am now 23 and the year is 1902. This is in London and my name is Elizabeth. Norma is my midwife."

Why do you have a midwife?

"I am carrying twins, two days due. I feel transfixed in this hallway."

I then moved her forward to the next significant event.

"I'm in the kitchen throwing up. Back pains, waddling around. An uncomfortable pregnancy. I am very big but not fat, heavy with twins, walking around in full gear and a hat. I'm in the drawing room now reclining and the pain in the womb is back. I have a constant feeling of sickness and I can't keep any food down. Everybody is worried, whispering around me.

I am offered tea now, don't want it. Breach birth, can't turn babies around."

What do you think will happen?

"I do not know, there is lethargy. I will it to go, but I have no strength."

At this point we left this lifetime for the time being. We were making no progress towards finding the actual moment that repressed the trauma and caused the fear of being ill and vomiting to manifest in later lifetimes. I thought there must be another element to this and perhaps we needed a catalyst, another energy.

For some reason I had an urge, perhaps intuitively, to ask her to find a person that she is very close to in her present life, her friend Jenny who is a very spiritual and intuitive healer and has been working with Pat. She had mentioned her a few times during our chats between hypnosis sessions. I'm not sure why at this stage I asked her to do this but it just felt right. It is as if we needed some help from somewhere. She found another door and went in.

"A white flowing gown like a priestess wears. She was my pupil once."

Where do you find yourself?

"I see a lot of lakes and woods. White light around us, starlight and moonlight."

If she was your pupil what did you teach her?

"The ways of the woods. Goddess. Looking around for a temple but there is not one. No, this is to do with being a Hedge Witch."

I asked that, with her help, can she find some herbs for Elizabeth.

"I ask her and she says lady's mantle and. thyme in a tincture. Lady's mantle for the womb and thyme for strength, and oak barks. Infusion.
This is a happy time here in this life and here she is my daughter."

What are your names in this lifetime?

"Hers is Bronwyn and mine is Eliza. I think we are somewhere in Europe and there are mountains and hills."

I then asked her to see the tincture being made and then bring it with her as she left this lifetime, thanking her past life daughter as she went. As she returned and entered the door where the ill Elizabeth was I asked her to imagine herself drinking the tincture as she became Elizabeth once more.

"I am crying in the bedroom and I see a window to the right. Subdued light. I am awfully tired. I see everything now and this is after the twins. As I drank the tincture I felt the sickness subside."

Tell me about the emotions that you feel

"I feel immense grief. I know that my life is ebbing away. I am haemorrhaging badly."

And what about the twins?

"I think they are dead. A boy and a girl. The girl may still be alive. It was Jenny again and she's the little girl. She may survive."

Tell me more about how you feel now that you have drunk the tincture.

"I feel I'm at one with the chair that I'm sitting in, earthed. Norma is coming back now trying to give me something. But I haven't got the strength."

I felt it important to release the emotions of the trauma of the birth so I asked her to return to the time just before the birth. I felt that with the energy of the healing tincture and the energy of her soul mate, Jenny, she would be able to face this now and allow the abreaction that we needed.

"Walking up and down in a lot of pain. Norma keeps making me walk, trying to turn the baby once more but she cannot. I am in labour for a long time, it goes on for days."

Tell me about the physical feelings that you are aware of.

"Screaming, raving, piece of wood in my mouth, squatting on bed. Breach is born (the boy). I tear and I can see the midwife taking the boy away, all blue with the cord around his neck."

And then what happens next?

"I rest, blood everywhere. I deliver girl. This is not so bad, she cries as I hold her. I take her to my breast, but I know I will die. Then comes grief, I have the girl on me and I feed while I'm bleeding empty."

She cries and really feels the sense of impending loss. I asked her then to leave this lifetime and reflect on her experience.

"I wasn't ready to leave my child and die. I was awfully sick but I feel very peaceful now. I was trying to block an awful lot of emotion but I feel I am free from it now."

*   *   *   *   *   *

I believe that in this case, using the Hedge Witch's medicine allowed her to face this blocked repressed trauma and bring it to the surface and let it go. Following this experience her fear of vomiting subsided.

I am also sure that her friend Jenny had a role to play here. She had already been having healing sessions with Pat and they were very evidently soul mates.

Because Jenny was her daughter in both of these previous lifetimes, this was the missing link we needed to connect in order to heal.

This is probably why they have met up again in this lifetime, to deal with this issue. Sometimes certain energies are needed.

There is yet another variation of these past life self-visitations and in this one you can actually revisit a past life to assist your previous self, interact with them and help them through a trauma. This could be yet another form of Reframing, but not always, as the therapist and client work together to make this interaction happen. This is a technique that would not be employed very often and as an example you could go back to a pre-visited past life, again as your third party self and forewarn your past life self of some impending danger or you could perhaps help to show the way if your earlier incarnation has become lost. This could also be a case of you playing the role of your own guardian angel and maybe you have experienced one of those moments of clarity back in that lifetime and felt the presence of a higher power guiding you. You would never know that it was a future spiritual facet of your own being that was helping you.

And we can twist it still further, after all this is a chapter all about the weird and wonderful. What if you regressed to a time when you were actually a ghost? You could return to that time as your present self and interact with your former earthbound spirit and help to guide that part of you home. This idea also treads on the toes of Soul Retrieval where broken fragments of your soul are located and retrieved. A ghost may well be a soul fragment.

If whatever you do now spins off into an infinite number of future lifetimes, the 'butterfly effect', then what about all those choices in your past lives. These can be explored as well in a therapy that I have developed and called the Alternative Outcome Technique. It involves regression to a point in a past life where an important choice was made, then exploring a different path with another row of doors to see what would have happened had the other choice been made. This technique is just as useful in a person's present life. Was that decision you made when you were twenty one the right one? If you are now wondering what on earth is the point of a therapy like this then please let me explain. If people are dissatisfied with their present lot they may blame it all on some wrong choice they made years ago. The anxiety of not knowing what might have been eats away at them adding to their discomfiture. This technique will show them what would have happened had they made a different choice back then. The important thing here is the fact that it doesn't matter if the alternative outcome was better, it is the knowing that puts the mind at rest. The alternative path may be a whole lot bleaker in some cases. To demonstrate this let's have a look at Grace's session.

Grace was not at all happy in her marriage. Her husband Danny was hardly ever there, at work all day, in the pub in the evenings, off on all sorts of adventures with his mates at the weekend. Grace hardly spoke to him these days, it was as if she was just there for Danny's convenience, cooking and cleaning. On the plus side Danny was the breadwinner and followed a dedicated career but although he earned a good wage Grace seldom saw evidence of it but at least the bills were always paid. Danny spent much of his earnings on beer and personal social interests, leaving Grace at home feeling like a pauper. She wondered if she should have said 'no' when Danny proposed to her all those years ago. After all they had already been together for four years and Grace was quite happy with that arrangement. The proposal was more of an ultimatum really, marry me or we are finished. Of course Grace eventually agreed but what if she hadn't, what if she had said no and ended it there and then?

I asked Grace to find the time when Danny suggested they get married. She set the scene and experienced that time again in her mind's eye and then I had her leave that point and find an alternative path that represented her life had she refused to marry.

*　　*　　*　　*　　*　　*

"I am wearing sheepskin slippers, baggy trousers and a jumper. I'm standing on lino in a kitchen which is old and not very good. I don't recognise this place. An empty purse lays upon the table beside my depression pills."

I then asked her to move forward to a point equivalent to the present time but still on this alternative path.

"The door I have to go through has a swing bridge. I'm through now, I'm falling as there is nothing in there, and I'm falling into oblivion."

I then had her go further back in time, still on this alternative path to a point of significance.

"There is some sort of party or gathering, a circle of people I have to see. It's a therapy group, I am not well. I feel despair, my physical body feels clogged up and nothing flows."

I moved her forward again to the most important significant event.

"I am disorientated, trying to get home, walking. I get hit, a vehicle, a truck. I didn't see it. That's it, over. I am gone and I feel quite relieved."

I had Grace leave the alternative outcome then and return the way she went and then to rest in her safe place which was a garden chair near the steps. I asked her to think about the experience she had just had and to compare what has actually happened with what could have. She said this:

"You have to have love in whatever form to nourish the soul."

In comparison with her alternative path her present situation was perhaps not as bad as she considered it to be. After all, even though Danny is hardly the most attentive husband in the world she is warm, dry, fed and has three wonderful children who are always there for her. One wonders where they were in the alternative life that she explored. To gain further insight and given that Grace was a very good subject and also a practising Medium and Clairvoyant I asked her to communicate with a higher power, inviting her spirit guide to come and talk with her there in the garden. This is what Grace relayed to me:

"I know him but he's in a different guise. He's smiling. He is my advisor who dots the "i's" and crosses the "t's". He is holding my hand now telling me not to worry, all is well. He tells me that the path I chose was for a reason and I survive because of my strength of character. I follow my gut instincts and must continue to do so. As for my future, I must concentrate on my work, be creative and love myself. My heart's desire is coming and I must not dwell, let go of things and people I do not need."

I think that this session was very beneficial for Grace, offering peace of mind with the knowledge that she was on the right path in life which, in turn, will lead her to the right future.

This is a good place to discuss one or two of the more extreme types of journey we could use to travel to our previous lifetimes, the 'themes'. This part of the voyage is totally symbolic using a language that helps the subconscious to understand where we are going. Most often I use the garden but we can employ anything we wish as long it has the correct structure. You could start off in a train station, this could be the safe place reached after going down steps from the roadway above. The train could pick you up and the subsequent stations it goes to could represent different eras, the appropriate year being written on the large sign at the edge of the platform.

Vehicles are always very adaptable for journeys to previous lifetimes, I have even sent one chap off in a camper van and I can't remember why now but it seemed appropriate at the time. Then there is the Delorean sports car, the gleaming silver dream machine from the film "Back To The Future", a ready-made time machine for those who wish it. Spaceships work well too, we send our clients onto the bridge of the craft, sit them down at a set of controls and they have a screen in front of them. They observe what data they see on the screen or adjust the controls to display a certain chosen date and then take off to visit that time. When they get there the door opens - and you can add a bit of dramatic lighting here with vapour and other special effects, if you like - and then they climb down the metal steps and become who they were back in that past life. It won't work for everyone of course, the more analytic among you will not be at all comfortable with the presence of a glowing silver spaceship on the edge of the mediaeval battlefield you have just found yourself in.

Another unusual phenomenon that occurs very rarely is something called Xenoglossy and this fancy word is used to describe the speaking of a foreign language by a person in regression. The other rule that applies here is the fact that the client speaks in a language that is unknown to them. Also it is usually an ancient dialect, quite often so antique that the so-called experts cannot recognise it. This could well be a language that has been discovered in the past and documented but if you have never heard it spoken then you are in the dark. What would the Egyptian hieroglyphics actually sound like? Exactly. The reason I am having a bit of a dig at the language experts is because they reject any Past Life Regression recordings featuring Xenoglossy as totally made up gobbledegook if they can't recognise it. One of our PLTA members had a wonderful recording of a client who regressed to ancient Egypt and the language sounded beautiful, with accurately repeated phrases. A CD of the regression was taken to the experts at the British Museum but the whole thing was just a folly as ancient languages evolve too much over time and unfortunately they couldn't lay their hands on a cassette tape made in 10,000 BC for their reference. Shame.

The good news is that more recent languages have been identified occasionally and they do link in with the eras of their associated regressions and, again, these are usually ancient dialects of our modern tongues. As I have said, this doesn't happen very often and I have personally never experienced one with all the thousands of people I have regressed.

Remote viewing is another very useful little technique. Developed by the American military during the cold war for spying purposes, it allows an individual's awareness to act independently from their body. This is basically a form of controlled astral travel and I have already mentioned remote viewing here and there. It is quite feasible to allow your consciousness, soul, self, call it what you will, to leave your body as, after all, it does that readily during near death experiences and it really is quite common when we die! You may remember that I suggested that our consciousness does not live inside our physical brain. Well this helps to prove the point. The reason I use it in past life work is mainly to enable the client to find an important location in the present time that they have found in their past life experience, they can just fly up into the air and ask their all-knowing Higher Self to take them to be place they want to find. This is a present time experience so they will see the topography differing in certain ways compared to the past life journey. As mentioned before, this can also be used for soul fragment retrieval. So what would be the purpose of interrupting a perfectly good past life experience to float up into the clouds? Location, location, location. Sometimes it is difficult to grasp where you are in the world when under regression, any number of factors can inhibit this. It can be important to understand where you are, especially if you have a karmic imbalance with a place rather than a person. You may even need to physically visit that place in your present lifetime in order to sort this energy imbalance out. As an example I had a client who regressed to a life as a Cornish tin miner. He had moved to Cornwall in his present life following an overwhelming desire to be in that part of the country. This often indicates some sort of task which needs to be fulfilled in the area to which you are drawn and it will involve a visit in person to the physical location. During his regression my subject found himself being crushed slowly to death underground in a collapsing tunnel. Although he got a name for the particular coastal tin mine he was working in it didn't mean that it would be easy to find as there are hundreds of these disused works all along the Cornish coast. We had a rough location and the name of the village where he lived. He also knew the direction in which he walked to work. At this point we employed remote viewing so that we could look down on the area and see where this mine was in relation to his village and the local geography. Luckily he recognised the coastline he saw from his vantage point, he had already explored it since he had moved to Cornwall, which was no surprise to me. All he had to do then was go and physically visit the exact location, sit and meditate there and rebalance his energy, or retrieve a missing soul fragment as it was in this case.

So why is this possible? He certainly didn't go remote viewing back in that past life. Actually he did if you think about it. He died in the mining accident and floated up out of his body and before he was drawn into the tunnel to the light he may well have seen the mine from above.

The main reason that we can do this exercise in the middle of a regression is the fact that we are working with the all-perceptive part of us and it knows no boundaries and is not stuck in the body like the lower self and sees the bigger picture.

One could compare the idea of remote viewing in a past life with the ability to visit a past life as your present self. We have actually already explored the idea of a person regressing back to a scene in a previous lifetime and observing themselves from a third party viewpoint. Past life remote viewing is therefore just a variation.

There are no limits to remote viewing as far as physical distance is concerned and if we really want to we can travel off to anywhere in the universe. Without the restrictions of the physical third dimension we are travelling in a very different way. Forget the speed of light, a mere pipsqueak of a speed at only 186,000 miles a second, we wouldn't get out of bed for that. No, the mother of all is the speed of thought. This works outside the realms of physicality and is in tune with the higher vibration spiritual world. You could think yourself to a little planet buzzing around our next nearest star in an instant, it would take four years travelling at 186,000 miles every second to lug your carcass there, also it wouldn't be much use to you anyway unless that little rock you landed on just happened to have the correct environment to keep you alive for more than a couple of minutes. With the speed of thought we can transport our consciousness anywhere we choose, our only limits are our knowledge of where to go.

You can have a go at remote viewing by using the exercise in chapter 8. Perhaps you can pop over to your auntie's house and see what she is watching on the telly, wait for the adverts, fly back home and give her a ring. Listen to her freaking out when you describe to her what she's wearing and what she said to the dog. Hours of fun!

Better still, whiz around the world in the right direction to get past all the time zones, thus projecting yourself into the future, grab the lottery results and … no, I'm only kidding, it won't work.

One thing that will grind proceedings to a halt is self-doubt. I mentioned this in chapter 1 and the main restriction will be you. A number of things can block a good past life experience and these can be preconceived expectations and misconceptions, spiritual beliefs, lack of trust and rapport with your therapist and doubt in your own ability. As soon as someone goes into hypnosis their subconscious is very open and sensitive to anything it is introduced to and, as we know, it will believe. We have to be careful that the subconscious does not suspect that we are having doubts or it will act accordingly and pander to our whims.

We need to leave these blocks behind.

I have developed a little exercise to make sure that you leave any of your doubts behind before you approach a past life. Most have enough faith to get to the safe place, usually the chair in the garden. Yes I know I could perhaps just once suggest something different but I like to use things that I know are reliable and will work every time, a Ferrari would be nice but it would never make it down our farm track. Anyway I digress again. We get to the safe place with no problems and now we need to be honest and accurately identify just what the cause of our trepidation might be. We imagine being presented with a pen and writing pad then encouraged to write down our doubts, one per sheet of paper. That's fine by the way, the more paper we waste the more trees we have to grow which is good is it not? More woods, more wildlife. I know, controversial but paper doesn't come from rain forests.

Once we have everything written down we are instructed to put the pieces of paper, our fears and misgivings, into a briefcase. At the beginning of the pathway which leads to the doors of our previous lifetimes there is a dustbin and that is where the briefcase is put. This sends a symbolic metaphor to the subconscious that all thoughts which would sabotage proceedings are locked away, they can have no power. If you do try some self-regression but doubt your abilities, then have a go at this little exercise before you look for a previous life.

Chapter Eight

Regress Yourself

As Past Life Regression can be regarded as a combination of the perfectly natural everyday state of hypnosis and the spiritually uplifting and relaxing discipline of meditation, we can easily do it for ourselves.

It is understood that all hypnosis is self-hypnosis, meaning that a therapist can't actually hypnotise anyone. Instead he or she guides individuals into self-hypnosis and to do that all they do is use a combination of words in the right order.

It follows then that it is just as easy for you to regress yourself if you remember the words and you can say them to yourself in your mind, or record and play them to yourself or better still, get a friend to read them for you.

The whole process must be structured in an exact way and the stages clearly understood, so let's refresh our memories:

1. Make yourself comfortable and close your eyes.

2. Focus on your breathing to start the relaxation process.
3. Relax the physical body.
4. Imagine yourself in a garden.
5. Imagine yourself descending steps.
6. Go to a safe place, perhaps a reclining chair.
7. Enter and explore a previous lifetime.

Let's have a closer look at the stages so that we can understand their purpose.

1. Close eyes.

This cuts out all visual stimulation from your surroundings allowing you to focus within. Just by doing this the process of hypnosis begins.

2. Breathing.

Yes, you have got to breathe!

No seriously, the point of focusing on breathing helps you to become aware of your body and as you concentrate on your body it helps you to relax it.

3. Relax Body.

The reason you relax the body is to allow it to rest while you go on your past life journey in your mind. Relaxation is the key to hypnosis just as it is for other disciplines such as meditation. You are asked to imagine all your muscles relaxing and releasing tension, working from the top down, or with some therapists the feet upwards, visiting each part of the body in sequence.

As you relax further your subconscious becomes more and more dominant and this helps the relaxation process even more. This happens because the subconscious will act upon whatever you ask it to do and this is called suggestion. So if a therapist suggests that you will drift deeper into the relaxing feeling, the subconscious will make it happen. When the body is feeling all heavy and relaxed we can then go on to the next stage.

4.   Imagined Surroundings.

You are then taken on a journey in your imagination and your therapist will use a symbolic language that the subconscious will understand and react to. No, I don't mean your practitioner will start spouting drivel, more a case of guiding you by your senses. You see things, hear sounds, smell, touch and feel the surroundings in your mind's eye. The whole idea of this is to focus more and more within and to show your subconscious where we intend to go.

5.   Steps.

Most journeys into hypnosis, or hypnotic inductions if you want to be technical, employ the use of stairs or steps and this is done to deepen the level of hypnosis. If you suggest to the subconscious that with every step down you will drift deeper then with every step down you will drift deeper.

6.   The Safe Place.

Now we establish a little resting place, a sort of halfway house where you can imagine resting and feeling safe and secure before you start exploring your previous lifetimes. It could be a sun bed in a garden, if you have just imagined a garden, or an armchair by a roaring log fire, it depends on the theme of the journey. We are slowly building the structure of the inner mind voyage and you will feel safe in the knowledge that if you get a little lost or confused when exploring your past lives you will always know your way back to the safe place and then, from there, back to normal consciousness.

7.   Exploring Past Lives

For the next part of the journey there are as many different ways of exploring your past lives as there are previous lifetimes to explore. It all depends on how you begin because it is always good to stick to the theme of the journey. If it is a garden theme you can imagine walking down a pathway towards your past lives or perhaps across a bridge. If you choose a building then perhaps you can go down a corridor. Just about anything goes as long as you follow the correct procedures.

To access a previous lifetime I prefer my clients to imagine themselves choosing a door from a row of many as, again, this gives some structure to the journey. As I nearly always use the garden-based theme it is nice and easy to suggest that my subject finds themselves on a pathway with a wall on one side. Built into the wall there are many doors. This pathway stretches away in front of them and the suggestion is made to the subconscious that the further they go down this path the further they go back in time. You go down the path back in time first of all passing all the doors representing your present life, counting down in reverse chronological order. Then you are seeing the doors which lead to your past lives. It is best to suggest that each door represents a year and that you have the particular year written on each door. A simple structure like this will build up confidence and familiarity, leading to a good experience.

Another popular theme is a library. After going down some stairs in some sort of a building, to deepen the level of hypnosis, you enter a library and choose a book about one of your past lives. Another variation is to find that one single book which is yours, showing all of your previous lifetimes, perhaps one per chapter or one per page. You can open the book and see a picture and then you let the image of that page grow and you then become part of it.

However you get access to your past lives you can now explore them. Remember that this is in your mind's eye, your imagination. You have to imagine and you have to trust your imagination. Try not to analyse anything such as date matching or the fashion you encounter because as soon as you start doing that you will invite your conscious mind to join the proceedings like an unwanted gatecrasher at a party, ruining the whole thing. No, just accept without question whatever it is you find yourself imagining. It is a bit like a dream, you are a participating observer and you have no idea where it will take you so you just let it happen.

Usually the first previous lifetime you visit is a practice one chosen by your subconscious to help you improve your skills but this is not always the case. Sometimes an enthusiastic subconscious will throw you in at the deep end making sure that this unique opportunity is not missed. This is what makes past life exploration so interesting both for the client and the therapist, as you never know what is going to happen and every single regression is unique.

It must be made perfectly clear that self-regression is for curiosity-based exploration only and should not be used for any therapy that may be required. It is not advisable for you to go charging off into your past lives with the intention of curing an issue you may be carrying. A qualified therapist must be consulted if you feel that you have past life issues which are affecting your life today.

Further on you will see some scripts for self Past Life Regression and you will find that they are arranged in a sequence designed to train your mind and improve your abilities. I do not recommend that you go blundering into a past life the very first time you try hypnosis. It takes time and patience to build up your skills, so the first script will take you as far as the safe place and the second one will bring you back out of hypnosis into normal conscious awareness again. It is really important to know the return journey as it has to be the exact reverse of the induction into hypnosis. A good structure will bring you back to normality nice and gently.

The third script will take you back into hypnosis, or the meditative state if the idea of being hypnotised still worries you after all I have said, and the fourth script will take you to a past life. The final script will show you the way back.

Please take your time and really learn the journey. The scripts are there to help you and to provide structure. Please, always stick to these guides as they are more than just some general instructions, it may not look like it but they are written using a very precise language that the subconscious mind will understand. So if you are going it alone without a script reading buddy or your own recording do your homework and learn well.

It is important to really get to grip with this process so I feel it is pertinent to summarize once more. As stated earlier I will of course be using a common theme throughout your self-regression and for those who have not guessed already it will be my most used one, the garden. Once you have relaxed your body you will be guided into a garden in your mind's eye. As your imagination is stimulated you become more and more focused on what is happening and the more focused you become the deeper the development of your hypnotic state. You are in touch with your subconscious at this stage so you will be experiencing the garden with your senses: seeing, touching, hearing, and smelling. No you won't actually smell, not any more than you might do already, I mean your sense of smell. You become more a part of the scene and a little less aware that you are in your reclining chair in your lounge or wherever. The steps will come next and you will have the understanding that, by descending these, this suggests to your subconscious that you are drifting deeper into the deep hypnotic state of relaxation. At each stage of the journey just pause awhile to really take in your surroundings, for instance when you are on the steps decide what they actually look like. On the first induction we go to the safe place, the nice and comfortable reclining garden chair or something similar if you prefer and when you rest here imagine how comfortable this chair is, imagine soft cushions and feel your relaxed body sink into them. Imagine how perfect it would be as the sun shines down on you making you feel drowsy, drifting deeper and deeper, deeper and deeper.

Hey! Where were you off to? We haven't started yet. There, see how easy it is to become hypnotised!

Once at the safe place you now have some options. If this is the first induction then the safe place is as far as you go and you have to retrace your steps and return to normal conscious awareness. If you are going in for the second time in order to explore a past life then you don't actually need to visit the safe place. As long as you know it is there and you can find it if you need to, should you lose your way, then it can be bypassed for the time being.

Let's go back to the start of your first journey once again, there is nothing like repetition to allow you to learn. You go to the safe place and then come all the way back, returning to the foot of the steps then counting yourself up from 1 to 10. The suggestion to the subconscious says that by the time you reach the top of the steps you are back to normality. Please practice the initial induction and return a few times before you proceed to the next stage.

The second induction leads you to a past life and you will find that it is quicker this time because your subconscious is learning. To begin, all you have to do is quickly scan your body to be aware of any tension and let it go, just think it away. Alternatively you can focus on muscular tension and breathe it away, relaxing on the out breath, drawing in the energy of relaxation on the in breath. Once satisfied your body is relaxed imagine yourself floating away into the garden taking your time to walk through it and then climb down the steps again. This process will create an even deeper feeling of relaxation. At the bottom of the steps just be aware of the safe place over to one side but for now, stay where you are. You now imagine yourself on a straight pathway which goes away into the distance in front of you. Imagine what you want this to be made of and how it feels as you walk along it. Have the idea in your mind that this path takes you back in time, the further you walk the earlier the time period. Beside the path to one side you see the garden wall and built into it are numerous doors. Sometimes these doors present themselves in all different shapes, colours and sizes or, depending on how your own subconscious likes to show things, they may be all the same. As you are going back in time the further down the pathway you go, it stands to reason that your starting point is the present time. The very first door you go past, therefore, represents the here and now in your present lifetime. The doors are there to provide an entry point into a period of time somewhere within your whole existence. For the sake of structure and accurate communication with your subconscious we normally make each door a year apart, so you can be fairly precise as each one can then be identified as a particular year. You are instructed to imagine that there are dates written on these doors so that you know where you are in time. However, to begin with you may not be able to see the dates but your subconscious may tell you what they are in some other way, perhaps a feeling or a quiet inner voice speaking to you. Before you start to walk past the doors associated with your previous lifetimes you can, if you wish to, access the earlier years in your present lifetime as many issues stem from present life childhood but be cautious here because if therapy is needed this is beyond the do-it-yourself regression.

Once past your present life doors you can now look for a door which has a past life behind it. Your subconscious or Higher Self chooses this for you so all you have to do is search. A certain door will stand out from the others, perhaps presenting as a different colour or shape or maybe even caught by a beautiful shaft of sunlight filtering through the trees on the other side of the path. When you find a past life door just take a while to study it taking note of its colour, shape, door furniture and the date which is written on it. By focusing like this it will help you to tune in to the experience you will have once on the other side. Time now to open the door and step through and before you throw yourself into a wonderful past life experience just make sure that you close the door behind you. Also it is important to be very aware that the door will always be available should you wish to leave the lifetime you are exploring. You will know that if you think it is there behind you, it will be. Turn and face it, open it and return to the pathway. If you do wish to leave in a hurry please make sure that you closed the door, I'll explain why later.

Assuming that you are not going to do a runner you move onto the next stage, becoming who you were. You go through a transition now and start to become aware of the body you are now in, a little like stepping out from one car and into another, you know how to drive them both but they feel really quite different. Use all your senses to feel this body, become aware of it and also be ready for the unexpected as you may now have changed gender or put on a few pounds or better still lost a few. Here in your imagination you are looking through the eyes of that person you once were and you will find that this is similar to how it feels when you are having a dream.

There is much to take in now so, again, we need to have a structure and every stage is very easy to remember, which is a good thing when you are self-regressing because to open your eyes half way through and fumble through this book for the next instruction is definitely not an option. Structure will help to guide you and help you remember what to do.

The next stage is to become aware of what you look like, you already have an understanding of how you feel and now you can switch to visual and have a look. Do just that and look down at yourself starting with your feet. See if you are wearing anything on your feet or perhaps you are barefoot or maybe you cannot see your feet because of a ridiculously large frock blocking your view. Slowly work your way up your body seeing what you are wearing.

Always accept what you observe without question, never analyse because that will wake up your conscious mind and if that interferes your regression is doomed. If the date on the door doesn't match your pantaloons, then so be it and there is an explanation for this but do not try to find the answers during your regression. You are a participating observer in your past life experience, you are not there to make sense of it as you can do that afterwards when you come out of hypnosis and reality catches up with you.

Now you will have a good idea of what you look like, the next thing to do is establish where you are and the simple and structured way to do this is to look back down at your feet and see what sort of surface you see yourself standing on. If you are standing that is, assume nothing. What you observe will give you some clues about whether you are inside or outside.

Incidentally, I will just mention something before we go any further. If you are really interested in what you are reading here, very focused and imagining every step that I am describing then the chances are that you are now in the middle of a Past Life Regression. Think about it, when you read about observing the clothes you saw yourself wearing what did you see? And what colour was your door?

Back to the journey now. You have established that you are either indoors or outdoors by seeing what you are standing on and the next thing to do is lift your gaze up to the horizon and allow all your surroundings to form. Observe and explore, letting the moments tick by, making mental notes of everything you see.

Sooner or later a sense of wisdom will kick in and you just know what is happening. Listen to that quiet inner voice, it is your subconscious speaking to you. Again, always accept what you imagine without question. Never let old grumpy, your conscious mind, become involved, that part of you is like those narrow-minded miserable sceptics and nobody likes a party pooper. If you find yourself in a muddy trench and feel that at any minute now you will hear a whistle and you will have to scramble out and charge at the enemy then that is probably what will happen. Let it play out just as in a dream and allow yourself to be taken.

Whatever happens during this part of a regression cannot be scripted because it is a unique experience, your own. I cannot advise you what to do minute by minute so it is up to you to move the story forward. One thing I can suggest you do is ask yourself some questions. Any request for information that you think in your imagination will invite a response from the all- knowing part of your mind, formerly known as Cuthbert. Ask yourself what your name is here in this past life, how old you are and what location you find yourself in. The answers should spring into your thoughts and as always you must accept whatever answers come to you without question.

Let yourself be taken forward as the story unfolds. If you just stand there waiting for something to happen then it is fairly likely that you will just stand there waiting for something to happen, you have the pause button pressed. Imagine doing something in the scene you are in, it is okay to do this because your subconscious is in control of the imagination so whatever you can imagine yourself doing, it is the right thing.

When you feel that you have had enough of the scene you are in you can either move on to another period of time within the life you are exploring or leave and perhaps look for another past life.

To move forward in time during a past life exploration just ask for it to happen. Even though you are in the middle of a regression and experiencing a previous lifetime as if you are there and it is happening right now, you still have the knowledge that you are regressing and you are sitting in your favourite chair in your front room and the cat has probably decided that it wants feeding and won't shut up. So you can still communicate with yourself effectively and ask to be moved on. Just imagine the scene you have before you fading away and then a new one reforming as you arrive at a new time period. Take a moment to readjust and then see what you are wearing now, where you are and how it feels physically and emotionally.

Remember always to work at this, you have to push your imagination, it is not a cinema inside your head.

At some stage within your journey in one particular life you may run out of steam, so you will have to leave. You must make the return journey back the way you came, don't just open your eyes. Certain things should be done in an exact sequence.

To use the analogy for those who are computer savvy you don't just turn it off at the wall, it has to do a complex closing down routine. As with the computer it is not the end of the world if you just open your eyes or pull the plug but it is not ideal and there could be a few minor consequences. The structure is there to allow you to detach from that earlier lifetime and correctly bring yourself out of hypnosis. If you just snap out of it half way through a regression then you have left doors open and also remained connected with that previous existence and also your subconscious mind. This could lead to unwanted intrusions within your everyday thoughts in the form of flashbacks or it may affect your dreams. None of this is a worry of course because nothing about regression is dangerous but there again it is not the best way to do things either, so always come back the right way.

If you ever do find yourself being quickly jolted back into conscious awareness before you are ready, just close your eyes again and imagine that you are back where you were and then leave by the original door that is there behind you, close it tight and return the way you came back up the path and then to the top of the steps.

Assuming that there are no highly charged traumatic experiences there to hurl you out of hypnosis just leave by the door which you used to enter that particular lifetime, close it properly and imagine yourself disconnecting from your former self and then it is a good idea to have a rest. And if you remembered to bring that flask of tea with you, now would be a good time. If you have just flipped back through a few pages to find a reference to the flask then you really haven't grasped my weird sense of humour. The idea of a small stop here is to help with reflection, understanding and reconciliation as you think about the experience that you have just had. I usually recommend that you find a bench to sit on outside the door that you have just left. Imagine sitting there and allow some words of wisdom just to flow into your thoughts and reflect on what you have learnt from your experience. You will be amazed with the gems of wisdom that you come up with as you give your subconscious the chance of some direct communication.

When you are ready you can move on by imagining yourself rejoining the pathway. The choice is yours, as always, you are in control, so if you feel you have the time and enthusiasm you can explore another past life by looking for a different door further down, or back up, the path. If you feel that you have done enough for the time being you can make your way back by retracing your steps. Head in the direction of the ten steps, passing all the doors and then count up to the present time. When you imagine yourself passing the final door you reach the steps. You won't have to go to the safe place at this stage but there are plenty of reasons to do this at other times. On climbing the steps you are returning to normal conscious awareness and your subconscious knows that you are effectively closing off your connection and walking away. Open your eyes, stare at the ceiling for a few minutes and then remember that you need to start cooking your evening meal. No, that last bit isn't mandatory; I wouldn't want to confuse anyone who is trying this exercise in the morning. There is a point to my reference about returning to normality though, getting on with the cooking or whatever, and it is to do with time. When you are in regression you become much less aware of normal time and the way it passes. You will be amazed at how much time has passed while you were in hypnosis. So yes, the tea will be late, the cat will be lying on its back with its legs in the air and you will have missed that phone call that you promised to make at a certain time. What can you do about it? Just plan to spend double the time that you initially thought would do the job. To give you an idea the first practice of the initial induction and return will take up to fifteen minutes. A second induction followed by a visit to a past life could take another thirty minutes and each additional life you decide to explore could eat up a further twenty minutes each, so just be aware.

Did I say? Practice is the key. Yes of course I did and I am happy to repeat it because it is so important.

The Many Faces of You

If this all seems a little daunting and you doubt your ability to remember everything that needs to be done, then don't worry because there are many ways to enjoy a regression experience other than seeing a therapist. You could record the scripts and play them back which is quite a good idea unless, like me, you are not too fond of the sound of your own voice. Alternatively you could have a friend read it all out to you. It would have to be a friend who would take it seriously though or neither of you would get past the giggles stage. Another alternative is to download an mp3 audio file and I would recommend the ones available at www.pastliferegression.co.uk. These are recorded by a guy called Andrew, someone not too dissimilar to myself! There are also CDs available here for the traditionalist. Actually it must be said that if you do listen to some sort of recording, whatever it may be, you will find that the use of headphones will enhance your experience, it gets right inside your head.

There are even more ways to find out about your past lives. As hypnosis is such a natural and straightforward thing to do you can actually be regressed by a therapist without being in the same room as them. No, that doesn't mean you hold a glass up to the wall while he shouts next door - I mean the telephone. What a marvellous invention. As long as you can hear each other it works just fine. The idea of this may make one or two therapists twitch a bit if they are from the client prodding fraternity but if they do think they need to manhandle their subjects to get results then they wouldn't offer telephone regression anyway. A video call using Skype is another way of doing things and if this appeals I would recommend the service offered at:

www.hypnotherapysouthwest.co.uk.

The therapist there is called Andrew Hillsdon, someone not unlike me.

And then of course you could use a surrogate. No, you won't need to ask someone to have a baby for you in order to find the cause of your water phobia. By surrogate I mean a stand in, someone else can who can take your place and be regressed by the therapist. The surrogate is an individual who has psychic abilities and they will have the ability to tune into the person whose previous lifetimes are being explored. So a therapy session takes place with a qualified practitioner and the psychic surrogate in the room. The client, whose lives are being explored, can go and have a nice pot of tea because they are not involved on a conscious or physical level. They may be slightly aware that their regression is taking place or they may not. If a trauma is uncovered and a big chunk of repressed emotion is released, they probably will. The psychic will usually tune in after seeing a picture of the client or holding an object that belongs to them or they may just have a few details such as name and date of birth. A recording or transcript is then sent to the client. This is a good way, for those who do not feel at ease in front of a therapist, to have a regression.

Finally you could have a reading. Many professionals are uncomfortable with this practice as it is completely non-client based, meaning that all the information comes from the psychic reader. These are clairvoyants, card readers and mediums. Personally I do not have any strong reservations about this because there are some wonderful and extremely gifted people providing this service. However, unless the information has come directly from you how would you really know if what they are saying is true? Quite often I have seen clients who have had readings and the information has been verified in regression so this is one way to validate a reader's credibility. This is a bit of a minefield really and there is probably quite a generous sprinkling of charlatan in amongst the talented ones. Having said all that, if a reading does appeal I can recommend that you go to www.pastliferegression.co.uk as there is a lady there who can offer this service, who is not entirely unrelated to me.

So, you have had a practice which is always good and you now have the ability to fall into a nice relaxed state at the drop of a hat and are able to access any past life, but then what? This is a little like learning to drive a car, passing the test then wondering where to drive. What can you actually do when you are in a past life? I am tempted to say 'anything you want' but that's not strictly correct as you have to go along with what is already recorded in your subconscious. It is time to go back to basics and think about the reasons you want to be regressed in the first place. Why do people approach a therapist for Past Life Regression? Curiosity accounts for about 60% of cases, I would say, and certainly there are many aspects of their previous lifetimes that they could be curious about. They may just want to see who they were and that is the obvious reason but it seldom happens in such a simplistic way. It is more a case that they want to see who they were because:

Because they have a deep interest in the history of America during the time of the Civil War and want to see if they had a life there.

Because they feel more at home in France than they do in the UK, they need to know if there is a connection.

Because the sound of the cannon fire they heard at a visit to a castle made them a quivering wreck, why?

What causes them to burst into tears when they've watched a film set in a certain era and location.

What is love at first sight all about?

The list is endless and every case has its own unique set of credentials and this is why a Past Life Therapist never gets bored, everyone they see brings them a new and exciting adventure.

So, before you close your eyes and embark once more on that incredible journey of discovery ask yourself why you are doing it, think of something pertinent to your own character that it would be beneficial to understand. Your subconscious can show you all sorts born out of its own choice but sometimes it is you, here in the flesh, your lower self that needs to know the answers. Your previous lifetimes have the capacity to give the answers to questions you may never think of so focus, concentrate and think of a question. Then as you walk past those doors with that question in your head your subconscious can work with the instructions and show you an answer. This is your time machine, so take control. If, for instance, you have a fascination for Angels ask to meet with them. If you wonder what happens when you die ask this to be shown. If a stranger whom you met at a party last week doesn't seem like a stranger at all, ask why.

Now let's see where all this has been leading. We need to follow a carefully written set of instructions or perhaps it would be better to call them directions. They are actually called scripts. These guides are carefully constructed in order to direct you and use a subtle language that your subconscious will understand. They are designed to fully engage your imaginative creative side employing elements that will involve your senses. Whilst feeling the warmth of the sun and smelling the flowers your focus sharpens and you become slightly less aware of your real surroundings, you know they are there but you are less bothered about them. You can't cut out reality altogether, you will still hear any noises around you and these can sometimes be amplified somewhat as your awareness actually heightens when under hypnosis. It is all about focus within your mind's eye. The phrase 'stick to the script' is very apt when it comes to hypnosis. If you don't then nothing horrible will happen but if you do then something great will happen.

Here is the first script, the initial induction using the garden theme, the series of dots indicate short pauses:

Close your eyes and the first thing we are going to do is to relax the body and then we will go on to relax the mind. So ... to relax the body ... the first thing to do is take a deep breath ... now just concentrate on your breathing for a few moments ... slow ... steady ... deep breaths ... because breathing is all-important to help your body relax ... and it also helps you to focus on your body and become aware of your body more and more ... and the tensions held there in the muscles.

Now allow your breathing to become normal and relaxed ... slow ... steady ... normal ... gentle ... rhythmic breaths ... and as your breathing becomes slow and gentle ... the next thing to do ... to help relax the body further ... is to look inside your forehead as if it was a screen and imagine on that screen the word relax ... just see the word relax ... concentrate on the word relax and become aware of those tiny little muscles in your forehead ... and the little bits of tension they hold onto ... just let that tension go ... feel those tiny little muscles release ...

We carry a lot of tension in the muscles from the everyday stresses and strains of life ... but by being aware of this tension ... we can let it go and allow the body to relax more and more.

So now bring this awareness down to your jaw ... feeling how tightly it is held together ... how clenched the teeth are ... feel your jaw loosen ... allowing it to drop slightly as it reaches its most natural, comfortable position ... free of stress and tension.

And as your jaw relaxes more ... take your awareness down onto your shoulders ... another area where we carry a lot of tension ... feel the shoulders loosen ... feel that tension just melting away.

Now ... as your shoulders relax more and more ... concentrate on the muscles on either side of your spine ...

letting those muscles soften ... allowing that tension to leave your body now.

And as you do this exercise you become aware of how heavy and relaxed your body is feeling as you just let the tension go. You feel your body just sinking down into the chair you are sitting in (or bed you are lying on etc.) ... let the chair (or bed, etc.) do all the work of supporting your body ... give your body up to the chair (or bed, etc.) as it rests completely.

And now to the chest ... and down to the stomach ... feeling more relaxed all the time ... further down to the pelvic area now ... and feel this wonderful wave of relaxation flowing down further ... to the thighs ... the knees ... calves and shins ... and on to the ankles and feet.

A wonderful feeling of relaxation is passing down through your body ... feel this feeling at your shoulders once more ... and bring it down your arms ... wrists ... and hands.

You are now beautifully calm and relaxed ... and from now on every time you hear the words calm and relaxed ... you will drift deeper and deeper into this wonderful feeling of relaxation ... every time you hear the words calm and relaxed ... you will drift deeper ... and deeper.

It is a lovely feeling being warm ... comfortable ... calm and relaxed ... and now as you allow your body to relax completely ... fully supported by the chair you are in (or bed you are lying on, etc.) ... just let it rest there ... as you now go on a journey in your imagination.

Just use your imagination and find yourself in a beautiful garden on a warm summer's day ... just imagine yourself standing here in this beautiful place ... the air is warm and still and the sun is shining ... imagine a beautiful clear blue sky ... and all around you here are wonderful flowers ... trees and shrubs ... become aware of the beautiful colours of the flowers ... smell the fragrance of the blossoms on that warm summer air ... watch little butterflies as they dance around ... their lovely coloured wings catching the sunlight ... and you can hear birds singing in the trees ... and in the background ... there's a gentle hum of insects.

And the feeling you get in this beautiful place is one of peace ... and tranquillity ... and this wonderful feeling causes you to drift deeper and deeper ... becoming more calm and relaxed as each moment passes.

And now ... as you stroll through this beautiful place ... taking in the sights and sounds of nature ... you discover some steps ... ten steps which will lead you down to a lower level in the garden ... Just imagine yourself standing at the top of these ten steps ... you can choose what they look like ... what they are made of ... how they feel beneath your feet ... In a moment you will walk down these steps ... and you will find that with each step you take ... you will drift deeper and deeper into this wonderful relaxing feeling ... with each step you take ... you will drift deeper and deeper ... and as you walk down the steps you will count them down in your mind.

Now make your way down the steps ... 10 ... 9 ... 8 ... feel a wonderful sinking down feeling with each step you take ... 7 ... 6 ... drifting deeper and deeper ... 5 ... drifting down and down ... 4 ... 3 ... 2 ... deeper now ... 1 ... and onto a lower level.

You are now in an even more beautiful part of the garden ... and over to your right is a comfortable ... reclining garden chair ... make your way over to this chair and settle yourself down ... and as you settle here, feeling so warm ... comfortable ... calm and relaxed ... you close your eyes ... feel the warmth of the sun on your face ... and drift away ... just drift away ... drift deeper ... drift deeper and deeper ... into a wonderful deep ... deep feeling of relaxation.

And now in this beautiful state of relaxation ... we have access to your subconscious mind ... and that part of you is willing and able to allow you to continue this journey to that part of you where your past life memories can be discovered.

I have mentioned before an alternative script which replaces the first part of the initial induction and provides the additional comfort of protection. It is down to personal opinion and peace of mind and some of the more spiritual practitioners believe it is vital to provide this cloak of safety. It certainly does no harm so if you would like to have this as your starting script then here it is:

Just close your eyes and take a few deep breaths ... slow steady deep breaths ... and now allow your breathing to become slow ... gentle ... and normal ... slow, steady, gentle, normal rhythmic breaths ... and as your breathing becomes slow and gentle ... you imagine a beautiful golden light forming above your head ... like a cloud of golden light ... and now as you gently breathe in, you imagine that golden light beginning to be drawn into you ... feel that happening now ... and as you take another breath in you are aware of the golden light being gently pulled into you further ... illuminating the inside of your head ... imagine it lighting up the inside of your head ... and as it gently touches the areas inside your head ... it relaxes ... releases tension and heals ... feel that happening now ... and now as you breathe in again feel that beautiful golden light ... that healing light being drawn down your neck ... illuminating the top of your spinal cord ... relaxing ... healing ... releasing tension ... now gently breathe in again and feel the beautiful golden light flowing down onto your shoulders ... illuminating the shoulders ... relaxing ... healing making you feel really calm and relaxed ... and now breathe in again and feel that golden light passing all the way down your arms and upper body ... feel it glowing inside ... relaxing ... healing ... and as you breathe in again the golden light passes down through your lower body ... lighting up all your internal organs ... healing ... releasing tension ... causing you to drift into a wonderful deep, deep feeling of relaxation ... the golden light ... this healing light passes down further now ... relaxing the thighs ... the knees ... calves and shins ... and gently flows down into the ankles ... and then the feet ... relaxing ... releasing tension ... healing ... Feel this beautiful glow all through your body causing you to drift even deeper and deeper into this wonderful feeling of deep relaxation ... and now, as you breathe in more of the golden light ... this healing energy, ... feel it push gently out of your body now ... surrounding your body in this beautiful relaxing healing light ... like a cocoon of energy surrounding you ... protecting you ... healing ... making you feel safe ... and as you feel wonderfully relaxed ... free of stress and tension so you drift deeper and deeper ... deeper and deeper ... and you now feel totally calm and relaxed ... calm and relaxed ... and from now on every time you hear the words calm and relaxed ... you will drift deeper and deeper into this wonderful deep relaxing feeling ... every time you hear the words calm and relaxed ... you will drift deeper and deeper.

Just use your imagination and find yourself in a beautiful garden on a warm summer's day ... just imagine yourself standing here in this beautiful place ... the air is warm and still and the sun is shining ... imagine a beautiful clear blue sky ... and all around you here are wonderful flowers ... trees and shrubs ... become aware of the beautiful colours of the flowers ... smell the fragrance of the blossoms on that warm summer air ... watch little butterflies as they dance around ... their lovely coloured wings catching the sunlight ... and you can hear birds singing in the trees ... and in the background ... there's a gentle hum of insects.

The Many Faces of You

And the feeling you get in this beautiful place is one of peace ... and tranquillity ... and this wonderful feeling causes you to drift deeper and deeper ... becoming more calm and relaxed as each moment passes.

And now ... as you stroll through this beautiful place ... taking in the sights and sounds of nature ... you discover some steps ... ten steps which will lead you down to a lower level in the garden ... Just imagine yourself standing at the top of these ten steps ... you can choose what they look like ... what they are made of ... how they feel beneath your feet ... In a moment you will walk down these steps ... and you will find that with each step you take ... you will drift deeper and deeper into this wonderful relaxing feeling ... with each step you take ... you will drift deeper and deeper ... and as you walk down the steps you will count them down in your mind.

Now make your way down the steps ... 10 ... 9 ... 8 ... feel a wonderful sinking down feeling with each step you take ... 7 ... 6 ... drifting deeper and deeper ... 5 ... drifting down and down ... 4 ... 3 ... 2 ... deeper now ... 1 ... and onto a lower level.

You are now in an even more beautiful part of the garden ... and over to your right is a comfortable ... reclining garden chair ... make your way over to this chair and settle yourself down ... and as you settle here, feeling so warm ... comfortable ... calm and relaxed ... you close your eyes ... feel the warmth of the sun on your face ... and drift away ... just drift away ... drift deeper ... drift deeper and deeper ... into a wonderful deep ... deep feeling of relaxation.

And now in this beautiful state of relaxation ... we have access to your subconscious mind ... and that part of you is willing and able to allow you to continue this journey to that part of you where your past life memories can be discovered.

The next script, the return follows straight on from the initial induction and together they create your first exercise which should be repeated a few times to improve your imaginative skills. Here is the return:

Now it is time to return ... It is important to always return the same way ... you leave the chair now and make your way back to the foot of the steps again ... the ten steps which will lead you back to normality, back to the present. In climbing to the top you will return to normal conscious awareness.

Make your climb now ... 1 ... 2 ... 3 ... 4 ... 5 ... mind and body slowly returning to normality now ... 6 ... 7 ... 8 ... 9 ... 10 ... mind and body fully refreshed and returned to normality.

When the first exercise is so familiar that it is boring, it is time to move on. This second segment consists of three stages with a script for each one but it is all done all in one go. The first is the second induction which will take you back to the bottom of the ten steps in a much quicker way. By practising you have trained your subconscious so it knows the journey very well, so now you can take a few liberties and employ one or two short cuts. Here is the next script:

Make sure you are comfortable and relaxed once more and close your eyes.

Once again take a few deep breaths and blow away any tension that you are aware of in your body ... just feel all those muscles relax once more as your body starts to feel calm and relaxed once again ... feel all that tension going ... this beautiful feeling of calmness is passing all through your body again ...

Now you are beautifully calm and relaxed ... calm and relaxed.

Imagine again that beautiful terraced garden ... that warm summer's day in this tranquil place ... stroll through the garden to the steps which lead down to the lower level.

In a moment, once more, you will walk down these steps, and with each step you take, you will feel more and more calm and relaxed ... with each step you take you will feel more calm and relaxed.

Now, make your way down the steps 10 ... 9 ... 8 ... 7 ... 6 ... getting calmer and calmer ... 5 ... 4 ... 3 ... 2 ... 1 ...

and onto the lower level ... you are now in that part of the garden where you find the chair.

And now at long last you can get to the interesting bit, your journey into your past lives. Please do not be put off by this seemingly boring practise because in reality there is very little to do and you will get to this stage in a very short time. The script, the past life journey, is the one which actually takes you to your previous lifetimes so learn this one well:

You needn't go to the chair now. Just know that it is there as a place of safety to return to, should you get lost or confused when exploring your past lives. Just find yourself on a pathway now which stretches away in front of you. As you look down the path, on one side you will see a row of trees and on the other side you will see a high wall. All along this wall you can see many, many doors.

Each door is an access to your past ... each door represents a year ... As you go down the path, the further you go, the further back in time you go. Each door has a number written above it showing you the year.

Now you make your way down the path, back in time ... Look at the numbers above the doors counting down as you go further down the path ... go past the nineteen-nineties ... the eighties ... the seventies ... ever onward. (Depending on your year of birth in this life) Go past the year you were born in this present life and go further and further.

Now you look for a door ... a door which stands out ... a door which has a past life behind it ... look for a door which stands out from the others ... one you are drawn to. Take a few moments to find one ...

See if you can see a number written above this door. Now you enter this door and once on the other side, close it behind you, but know it will be right behind you at any time should you wish to leave and return to the pathway.

Now you can explore this past life unscripted and when you are done the final script brings you all the way back to normal conscious awareness and it's simply a return journey. Make sure that you are also familiar with this one as it is just as important to return correctly:

Whilst still in past life:

Let those images fade now and you become aware of the door that is behind you that you used to come into this life ... turn and face it ... open it ... and step back out onto the pathway there in the garden ... closing the door tightly behind you making sure it is properly closed.

(You can do one of two things now. You can look for another door, another life, or if you have finished exploring continue with this)

Make your way back up the path in the direction of the chair and the steps and as you walk up the path bring back with you only those memories which you wish to keep and thank your subconscious for providing you with this insight into your past ... make your way up through the years into the 1900s now (depending on the date of the life you have just left) ... up to the 1950s now ... the 60s ... 70s ... past the 1980s now and into the 1990s and finally past the last door (present year) and make your way over to the foot of the steps.

It is up to you what you do with these scripts, whether you read them through a sufficient number of times in order to memorise them or you have someone read out loud to you. Alternatively you could record yourself reading them and then play the recording back to yourself.

You may already be bored to death with my beloved garden theme so let's freshen it up a bit and consider some alternatives. Probably the next easiest to learn is The Building where you find yourself on the flat roof of a tall building surrounded by breathtaking views. In one corner there is a little raised building with a door and this is your access. Once through the door you can find a set of stairs leading down to a lower level and this is your deepener now, just like the steps in the garden. Ten steps down you find yourself in a wide hallway, a sort of foyer with a little seating area off to one side. This is your safe place and you choose a comfortable arm chair, perhaps a recliner and settle down here in front of a roaring log fire and drift into a deep state of relaxation. For the next stage, the journey to your past lives, you leave the chair and make your way down a very long corridor and the doors you find there provide access to your previous lifetimes. Here are some scripts for the building theme:

Close your eyes and the first thing we are going to do is to relax the body and then we will go on to relax the mind. So ... to relax the body ... the first thing to do is take a deep breath ... now just concentrate on your breathing for a few moments ... slow ... steady ... deep breaths ... because breathing is all-important to help your body relax ... and it also helps you to focus on your body and become aware of your body more and more ... and the tensions held there in the muscles.

Now allow your breathing to become normal and relaxed ... slow ... steady ... normal ... gentle ... rhythmic breaths ... and as your breathing becomes slow and gentle ... the next thing to do ... to help relax the body further ... is to look inside your forehead as if it was a screen and imagine on that screen the word relax ... just see the word relax ... Concentrate on the word relax and become aware of those tiny little muscles in your forehead ... and the little bits of tension they hold on to ... just let that tension go ... feel those tiny little muscles release ...

We carry a lot of tension in the muscles from the everyday stresses and strains of life ... but by being aware of this tension ... we can let it go and allow the body to relax more and more.

So now bring this awareness down to your jaw ... feeling how tightly it is held together ... how clenched the teeth are ... feel your jaw loosen ... allowing it to drop slightly as it reaches its most natural comfortable position ... free of stress and tension.

And as your jaw relaxes more ... take your awareness down on to your shoulders ... another area where we carry a lot of tension ... feel the shoulders loosen ... feel that tension just melting away.

Now ... as your shoulders relax more and more ... concentrate on the muscles on either side of your spine ... letting those muscles soften ... allowing that tension to leave your body now.

And as you do this exercise you become aware of how heavy and relaxed your body is feeling as you just let the tension go. You feel your body just sinking down into the chair you are sitting in (or bed you are lying on etc.) ... let the chair (or bed, etc.) do all the work of supporting your body ... give your body up to the chair (or bed, etc.) as it rests completely.

And now to the chest ... and down to the stomach ... feeling more relaxed all the time ... further down to the pelvic area now ... and feel this wonderful wave of relaxation flowing down further ... to the thighs ... the knees ... calves and shins ... and on to the ankles and feet.

A wonderful feeling of relaxation passing down through your body ... feel this feeling at your shoulders once more ... and bring it down your arms ... wrists ... and hands.

You are now beautifully calm and relaxed ... and from now on every time you hear the words calm and relaxed ... you will drift deeper and deeper into this wonderful feeling of relaxation ... every time you hear the words calm and relaxed ... you will drift deeper ... and deeper.

It is a lovely feeling being warm ... comfortable ... calm and relaxed ... and now as you allow your body to relax completely ... fully supported by the chair you are in (or bed you are lying on etc.) ... just let it rest there ... as you now go on a journey in your imagination.

Imagine now that you find yourself on the flat roof of a building. This roof is very large and there is a wall around the edges which makes you feel perfectly safe ... beyond the wall you can see breathtaking views of the surrounding countryside ... just slowly turn around and take in this beautiful scene.

At one corner of this roof is a small square raised building with a door ... just make your way over to this door ... open it and walk inside ... you now walk onto a soft, thick-piled carpet ... you can choose the colour.

In front of you there are some stairs ... there are ten steps leading down ... in a moment you will imagine yourself walking down these stairs and with each step you take you will feel more and more calm and relaxed ... with each step you take you will feel more and more calm and relaxed ...

Make your climb down now ... 10 ... 9 ... 8 ... 7 ... 6 ... drifting deeper and deeper with each step you take ... 5 ... 4 ... 3 ... 2 ... 1 ... and step onto the floor of a beautiful hallway ... and over to your right is a big comfortable armchair beside a roaring log fire ... make your way over to the chair and settle yourself down ... as you sink into the chair ... listening to the gentle crackle of the fire ... just close your eyes and drift deeper and deeper ... drift deeper and deeper...

The initial return for this script is just as you would expect it to be and, again, if you choose this journey over the garden one please practise these first two scripts quite a few times before proceeding to the next stage.

Now it is time to return ... It is important to always return the same way ... you leave the armchair now and make your way back to the foot of the stairs again ... the ten steps which will lead you back to normality, back to the present. Make your climb now ... 1 ... 2 ... 3 ... 4 ... 5 ... mind and body slowly returning to normality now ... 6 ... 7 ... 8 ... 9 ... 10 ... mind and body fully refreshed and returned to normality.

I have also mentioned the library theme and this can be regarded as a variation to the building as they both start off the same. Instead of going to the safe place beside the log fire you enter the library at the foot of the stairs. The library itself can be regarded as your safe place and the books are your past life access points. Here is the script if this theme appeals:

Close your eyes and the first thing we are going to do is to relax the body and then we will go on to relax the mind. So ... to relax the body ... the first thing to do is take a deep breath ... now just concentrate on your breathing for a few moments ... slow ... steady ... deep breaths ... because breathing is all-important to help your body relax ... and it also helps you to focus on your body and become aware of your body more and more ... and the tensions held there in the muscles.

Now allow your breathing to become normal and relaxed ... slow ... steady ... normal ... gentle ... rhythmic breaths ... and as your breathing becomes slow and gentle ... the next thing to do ... to help relax the body further ... is to look inside your forehead as if it was a screen and imagine on that screen the word relax ... just see the word relax ... Concentrate on the word relax and become aware of those tiny little muscles in your forehead ... and the little bits of tension they hold onto ... just let that tension go ... feel those tiny little muscles release ...

We carry a lot of tension in the muscles from the everyday stresses and strains of life ... but by being aware of this tension ... we can let it go and allow the body to relax more and more.

So now bring this awareness down to your jaw ... feeling how tightly it is held together ... how clenched the teeth are ... feel your jaw loosen ... allowing it to drop slightly as it reaches its most natural comfortable position ... free of stress and tension.

And as your jaw relaxes more ... take your awareness down onto your shoulders ... another area where we carry a lot of tension ... feel the shoulders loosen ... feel that tension just melting away.

Now ... as your shoulders relax more and more ... concentrate on the muscles on either side of your spine ... letting those muscles soften ... allowing that tension to leave your body now.

And as you do this exercise you become aware of how heavy and relaxed your body is feeling as you just let the tension go. You feel your body just sinking down into the chair you are sitting in (or bed you are lying on etc.) ... let the chair (or bed, etc.) do all the work of supporting your body ... give your body up to the chair (or bed, etc.) as it rests completely.

And now to the chest ... and down to the stomach ... feeling more relaxed all the time ... further down to the pelvic area now ... and feel this wonderful wave of relaxation flowing down further ... to the thighs ... the knees ... calves and shins ... and on to the ankles and feet.

A wonderful feeling of relaxation passing down through your body ... feel this feeling at your shoulders once more ... and bring it down your arms ... wrists ... and hands.

You are now beautifully calm and relaxed ... and from now on every time you hear the words calm and relaxed ... you will drift deeper and deeper into this wonderful feeling of relaxation ... every time you hear the words calm and relaxed ... you will drift deeper ... and deeper.

It is a lovely feeling being warm ... comfortable ... calm and relaxed ... and now as you allow your body to relax completely ... fully supported by the chair you are in (or bed you are lying on, etc.) ... just let it rest there ... as you now go on a journey in your imagination.

Imagine now that you find yourself on the flat roof of a building. This roof is very large and there is a wall around the edges which makes you feel perfectly safe ... beyond the wall you can see breathtaking views of the surrounding countryside ... just slowly turn around and take in this beautiful scene.

At one corner of this roof is a small square raised building with a door ... just make your way over to this door ... open it and walk inside ... you now walk onto a soft, thick-piled carpet ... you can choose the colour.

In front of you there are some stairs ... there are ten steps leading down ... in a moment you will imagine yourself walking down these stairs and with each step you take you will feel more and more calm and relaxed ... with each step you take you will feel more and more calm and relaxed ...

Make your climb down now ... 10 ... 9 ... 8 ... 7 ... 6 ... drifting deeper and deeper with each step you take ... 5 ... 4 ... 3 ... 2 ... 1 ... and step onto the floor of a beautiful hallway ... in front of you now is a big heavy wooden door ... open the door and walk into a large room which you can now see is a library. All around you are many, many books ... all these books represent your past ... volumes and volumes showing the story of your many previous lifetimes.

Every book is clearly marked ... some may have a year written on them ... others may have a title.

Now look along the shelves and choose a book ... one which stands out from the others ... one you are drawn to ... now take the book and lay it on a table which you find there in the centre of the room ... now look at the book you have chosen and before you open it, become aware of the outside cover ... see what picture or words there are here.

Now it is time to open the book ... you will see there are many pictures there to observe ... choose a page and become aware of what you see.

Now ... let the picture grow ... growing bigger ... so big now that you can step into that picture ... step into that picture now ... into that life ... be part of it ... finding yourself in a different body now ... looking through the eyes of the person you now are ... the scene forms stronger and stronger around you now.

Investigate your chosen past life as you would with the other themes. When you have finished exploring proceed as follows:

Let those images fade now and become aware that you are stepping out of this life ... stepping out of the book ... finding yourself in the library ... and now you can look back at the book ... seeing the scene you have just left as a picture in the book ... so just close the book and put it back on the shelf.

After this you can choose another book, another life or return to normality:

It is time to leave the library now ... so make your way to the large wooden door ... open it ... walk through and make sure you close it behind you ... now it is time to climb the stairs back to normality ... make your climb now ... 1 ... 2 ... 3 ... 4 ... 5 ... mind and body slowly returning back to normality ... 6 ... 7 ... 8 ... 9 ... 10 ... fully refreshed ... fully back to normality ... and when you feel ready you can open your eyes.

Of course there are many other ways to visit a past life and there are some practitioners who prefer to completely cut out all these gently structured themes and just say "Go back to a past life now, take your mind back (clicks fingers) you're there! First impressions! Is it light or dark, warm or cold, what's the first thing you see?"

Well if that floats your boat all well and good but personally I believe that this sort of approach is quite intimidating and creates a form of panic. All this clicking fingers, banging on the desk and excessive prodding and tapping of the forehead is not for me. I think you should enjoy your experience rather than feel like a new army recruit on parade drill.

If you want to play around with some different ideas and themes then you can experiment and make up your own. Some of my clients even sneak off and do their own thing while I am regressing them, perhaps adding a river beside the garden or construct a beautiful fountain beside their safe place. I even get requests - they would prefer a beach perhaps. If that happens I am only too happy to oblige because the same old wander through the garden can be lovely for them seeing it for the first time but I have already been there a few thousand times. In fact it is so automatic now I can find myself saying the words yet having little input at the same time and this is another subconscious function, if you do something often enough the subconscious switches to autopilot and does it for you. So, if they want a beach they can have a beach. As long as there is a structure then the world is our oyster. We can start on the cliff top, climb down steps built into the rocks, create a safe place on the sand and then go and find a row of caves which lead to their previous lifetimes. If you are into sci-fi, the Time Machine may suit you well and here is a script for it starting from the safe place, the chair in the garden so you obviously have to go as far as the second induction before this next bit:

Leave the chair and make your way across the garden. Beyond the edge of the garden you will find a clearing ... and in this clearing is a large, shiny, silver spaceship. This is a very special vessel ... a time machine. You will have full control over this machine ... finding the controls easy to use ... and it will take you to wherever you wish to go in your past.

As you approach the time machine ... this beautiful silver ship ... a set of steps lowers down for you.

Now you climb into the ship ... and now you are at the top of the steps ... And you go inside the ship ... you see a captain's chair in front of a control panel. Make yourself comfortable in the chair and familiarise yourself with the controls. There is a screen in front of you and a number pad below this. To the right of the number pad is a lever.

You are in control of the journey that this time machine takes you on, and all you have to do is to press the numbers ... choosing a date ... a year. Your inner mind knows which year you are going to choose ... and it will help you press the right numbers now. See yourself pressing the numbers, watching them appear on the screen in front of you. You press four numbers to make a date, a year. You become aware of the year you will visit as you see the number on the screen.

Now the controls are set to take you to this year ... and to make the machine move to this year all you have to do is pull that lever backwards towards you. Pull the lever now and feel the machine start to move ... you may have sensations of movement and of sound as the machine takes you back in time. And now as the machine settles again the engines shut down and all is quiet and still. You become aware of the steps lowering down once again, and as you now make your way down the steps you become the person in this previous lifetime ... looking through the eyes of this person ... feeling yourself in the body of this person. Also, just know that this machine will be behind you whenever you wish to leave this past life. All you have to do is to turn around and walk back up the steps into the time machine.

Proceed as with any other regression. The return or onward journey to different lifetimes is very straightforward. You just set the controls once again for another date in another life, or if you wish to return to normal conscious awareness set the present date and return to the garden where the safe place is. You disembark and return to normality up the steps in the normal way.

We looked at remote viewing earlier on and this is another one that you can try at home. As with all things you need to practice. Why you should wish to do this and where you would choose to go is your business, so if you want to give it a try here is a script for it:

Starting off from the safe place, the chair in the garden or wherever:

Imagine yourself ... gently feeling a pull upwards ... an energy just pulling you upwards. Feel your consciousness being pulled up now away from your physical body.

As you look down now ... you become aware of your physical body ... see it below you.

And you start to move higher now ... away from your body ... seeing it below you ... seeing the countryside below you now.

Higher still ... you can make out the shape of the landscape below you ... recognise the shape of the land.

And now ... as you think of your destination ... you feel yourself moving off in a certain direction ... moving towards your destination ... moving more quickly now ... watching the land below you.

And as you feel yourself nearing your destination ... you start to descend ... the land below you grows larger and the details become clearer ... lowering down to the ground now ... reaching your destination.

Become aware of where you find yourself ... look around and observe what you see.

The return journey is just a reverse of the above.

Finally the other exercise that you can do for yourself is the Future Choice Meditation. This is to do with making decisions and if you do find yourself in a position where an important decision has to be made, one that will shape and change your life, this will help you make up your mind.

The Many Faces of You

Your Higher Self knows what the right path to take is and as you take yourself on the Future Choice Meditation journey you will give it the opportunity to point you in the right direction, maybe not necessarily the path you feel you want to take but the right one for your journey through life. This exercise can be adapted to any form of decision you are faced with, whether it is a change of job or partner or just which outfit you wish to buy. All you have to do is imagine a signpost that has your choices written upon it. This is a simple journey and although there is a script to guide you, let your imagination work as you explore the different directions. Here is the script:

Start from the safe place. Once again it is best to choose a garden or something similar with an outdoor theme.

Leave the chair now and walk behind it ... and on the other side of the garden you can see a wide pathway. This pathway leads you out of the garden and into woodland.

This is a pleasant wide open pathway through the woods ... the sun is shining down on you and you feel comfortable, calm and relaxed.

As you walk along this pathway think about the choices that you have and of the decisions that you wish to make.

The pathway now leads you to a T-junction and as you approach the T-junction ... you see a signpost there and the signpost points to the left and to the right ... The two directions here represent your two alternatives and you can explore each direction to allow your mind to symbolically show you which feels the right way to go. As you look at the signpost you see words on the signpost symbolising the choices that you have.

So look at the signpost now and become aware of what the two directions are called.

And now choose which direction you would like to explore first.

Now make your way down in this direction ... in the direction indicated (your 1st choice) ... and as you go down this pathway you become aware of how this feels and what you see. Be aware of all feelings, emotions and the energies that you find in this direction.

Now look for something special ... a symbol of some sort. Find something that your mind will show you now ... that will help you understand whether this is the right direction for you or not. Look for this symbol now ... it could be anything. Become aware of when you have found it.

Become aware of what it means to you.

The Many Faces of You

Now turn around and walk back along this path, back to the T-junction where you find the signpost. Make your way up the path and become aware of when you have reached the signpost.

And now it is time to walk in the other direction, in the direction of (your other choice). Make your way now down in this direction ... in the direction of (your other choice). Become aware of how it feels walking in this direction ... your feelings and emotions. Be aware of what you see around you.

And now once again look for a symbol ... a symbol which represents this direction. Something ... an object that will help you understand the nature of this direction ... this choice. Become aware of when you have found it

And now it is time to return once again ... and you are returning now, back to the T-junction with all the knowledge that you need for the choices that you can now make. Become aware of when you have reached the T-junction and are by the signpost once again.

Now that you have explored the two alternatives ... you can make a decision. Become aware of what the decision is.

And now it is time to return back up the main path through the woods towards the garden and the comfortable reclining garden chair ... your safe place. Make your way back along the pathway ... approaching the garden, ... into the garden now and back to the comfortable reclining garden chair.

One of the many reasons to have a regression is to find out if you had shared previous lifetimes with people you know now in your present life and there is a very easy way to find this out. The first thing you will need to do is ask to be directed to any past lives where you have been with a certain individual, so to do this you have to think about the person as you commence your journey down the path, passing the doors. Just think these words: "If I have shared previous lifetimes with Jenny please show me a door now", knowing that behind the door you will experience a past life where you can find this person. If, of course, the person you are looking for is not called Jenny … well done, you are ahead of me now. Back to serious mode, please note that you have to use the word if. It is imperative that you do not entice your inner mind to produce something suggested to it that didn't exist. This way you will only see the door if you did actually have a past life with the person you are looking for. The subconscious will imagine something false if you suggest that it could. Once you have been presented with a door or, should I say, if you are presented with a door then you will know that you will find the person you are looking for in the past life that sits behind it. On entering that past life you may not necessarily stumble upon Jenny (or a person of your choice) straight away. Your subconscious may decide to set the scene first so that you can gain a greater understanding of your roles in this particular lifetime. When you do encounter your sought after counterpart you may recognise her or him straight away even though their appearance is quite different. Alternatively you may only have the slightest inkling that the person you find yourself interacting with could be the one you are looking for. To help you to confirm this all you have to do is look straight into their eyes, which helps you to connect with their soul and if this is the person you seek, knowledge will come to you as your subconscious confirms this.

Another way to do this would be to let the images that you have in your mind just fade away and then ask to be shown a scene where you are totally alone with the individual you are looking for. This will clear away any doubt. You may also have shared many other lifetimes with this person and you can leave the lifetime you are exploring and ask it this is the case and, if so, please show another door. Remember to use the word IF. On visiting a few previous lifetimes shared with your friend, partner or whoever it is, you may well see certain karmic patterns emerging which in turn will help you understand your interrelationship in your present lifetime. For those who don't have time to recall all these other shared lives and just want to know how many there were, just ask. To do this it is best to return to your safe place and ask to be shown the answer to your question in some graphic form; you could imagine picking up a book from your newly imagined picnic table and know that when you open it there will be a number. That's how many lives you have shared with Jenny.

We have now covered all of the various exploration-type journeys that can be done with self regression but there are still some more experiences to have at your safe place.

This is the perfect meeting place as it is deep enough as far as Hypnosis and meditation are concerned thus creating a raised vibration, yet not to a point where you are totally engrossed in a Past Life Regression.

Most of the reasons to have meetings here are related to therapeutic needs and are therefore unsuitable for self-regression. We can, however, arrange a few interactions with the many forms of being who reside in the higher vibrational realms of the spirit world. Some of these have already been mentioned in previous chapters but it is worth reiterating here. It could be a spirit guide, a loved one or a close friend who has passed over, karmic partners as discussed previously or even parts of you.

Let's have a look at spirit guides to begin with. We have discussed these earlier and there are many benefits in being able to communicate with our

The Many Faces of You

guides in such an precise way. They are never very far away to help steer you in the right direction through life, a little nudge here and there to keep you on your chosen path. They watch over us, but not in a being stared at when sitting on the toilet sort of way, they work on more subtle levels.

If you want to meet your spirit guide just ask him or her to join you. Have a second chair set up beside you, imagine it being there before they arrive otherwise your faux pas of not providing a seat for your guest could cause some embarrassment. I've made a reference to their gender here as this is usually how they will present themselves, as male or female but in reality as spirit beings they are androgynous but as I have said before they nearly always choose to show themselves in the same guise and appearance as they looked in one of their own former incarnations. Each lifetime we have resonates at a certain frequency or vibration and infused within that energy will be the wisdom gained during that lifetime. As an example many guides appear as Native American Indians, a very wise race indeed and in tune with the spirit realms so very suitable for guide duty.

A meeting with your guides will help you to understand their roles and the more you practice the exercises in this chapter the easier your communication with your helpers becomes. In fact when I was in a meditation circle on a regular basis which also taught various healing techniques, I found I was just able to feel the presence of my guides whenever I elected to tune into them. When your guide joins you at your special meeting place you have a wonderful opportunity to ask all those questions about life, the universe and everything, questions that only a being from the other side could possibly answer. What you do ask is entirely up to you but I would suggest it is something pertinent to your life and destiny rather than what you can have for your tea. One important thing you must do here is to learn to be a good listener as guides communicate in a way that has grammatical differences so it is sometimes difficult to grasp the exact nature of the messages you are seeking. Listen well, remember well and spend time ruminating over the information you have been given.

A meeting with angels is slightly different again. These are the more advanced beings, higher up the hierarchy scale. Rather than imparting gentle wisdom they are more likely to bless you with some form of gift such as good health, intuition or protection from entities. Angels appear to have a variety of specific roles so just accept whatever is offered, it's their particular thing. Some spiritually-minded people consider guides and angels to be one and the same thing, or suggest you have a number of angels to help you through life. I feel more comfortable with the idea of a hierarchical structure; this seems to be the way of things.

The Many Faces of You

Then we have top brass, the big cheeses of the angel world, the archangels. These omnipresent characters are all well known to those in the know and they are called upon by psychics and healers for their individual expertise. It is not common to have a one-to-one with these guys but you never know.

Other souls that you have the opportunity to meet are the ones who have been part of your present life in days gone by, but have now been sadly parted from you as it was their time to leave their earthly bodies and return home. A meeting with someone who has been close to you but has now died can be very therapeutic and can help you with the grieving process. Certain things left unsaid at an untimely death can now be said and it is comforting to know that a loved one is safe and happy.

When you start to organise your meeting place you can be safe in the knowledge that whoever you call upon to join you, they will turn up. They are never too busy. We do not need a script for safe place meetings and this is because the first bit is simple, just provide a chair and give out a call. The second bit cannot be scripted because it is a totally unique experience for each and every one of us. You can say what you want, ask what you want and then listen to the answer. Trust that you will understand what you are told and also be aware of the fact that they may communicate in different ways, such as telepathy or showing you pictures.

Finally let's have a little recap on a whole past life journey. I know I repeat things but that is how we learn.

However you choose to do this, by seeing a therapist, listening to a CD or just memorising the journey and doing it yourself, you will first need to create a comfortable environment where you won't be disturbed. There is nothing worse than hearing a telephone ring when you are just entering a castle on your horse!

You can lie down on a bed, on the floor, on a reclining chair, or sit if you prefer. You can glue yourself to the ceiling if you like just as long as you make yourself extremely comfortable.

Next you close your eyes in order to cut out visual stimulation from your surroundings and then concentrate on your breathing. This helps to relax the body and to focus on it. Imagine yourself breathing away muscular tension as you exhale and replacing it with the energy of relaxation as you inhale.

Taking your time, gently work your way through your physical body concentrating on each part in sequence, letting the tension go and relaxing more and more.

Use your imagination now as you focus in your mind's eye. It is best to stick to a theme such as a garden. Explore your chosen scene using all your senses.

Now you find some steps of some kind, knowing that when you climb down them you will relax even further.

Establish a safe place such as a reclining chair or a shady spot under a tree.

Continue the journey to the area where you can enter a past life, perhaps through a door or after walking over a bridge.

Explore the past life in your imagination.

Leave and retrace your steps. It is important to close any doors have opened and to climb any steps that you have descended.

Open your eyes and go "Wow!"

Chapter Nine

Final Thoughts

As we now reach the final chapter it is time to reflect on what you might have gained from this book. It may have helped you understand the workings of regression and dispelled all those misconceptions about this therapy that prevent so many people enjoying the experience. You may have gained a little more knowledge about the spirit world. Perhaps I have helped you onto a spiritual path of self-discovery, a stepping stone within your evolution.

Maybe you think I'm a total head case and talk absolute nonsense - it didn't stop you reading this to the bitter end though did it?

Whatever my words have done for you hopefully it has set you thinking about the bigger picture and your part within it. I would not expect you to accept every word as gospel and there are bound to be a few controversial areas that you are not at all comfortable with but that's fine, I have never stated that I know it all. So put some of it in your recycle bin, more on the back burner and run with what you still carry.

My interest in past lives has helped me carve a career in this field and I have gone to great lengths over the years to bring Past Life Regression to a greater audience. This was the main reason for starting The Past Life Therapists Association back in 2001 so that like minded therapists could get together and be recognised as specialist practitioners rather than Hypnotherapists who just do a bit of past life work as well. The association offers membership to any therapist who holds the necessary credentials so they do not have to be exclusively trained by ourselves. We are strict on this though and all applicants have to verify their qualifications. This is why we can endorse all our members with confidence, knowing that clients who approach us will be in good hands.

The association has a fairly large web site, something over 400 pages some of which only the students that we train will see. The majority of the membership fees are invested in advertising and you will always find us in the most prominent positions on all the major internet search engines.

We have quite a few web addresses but the main one is www.pastliferegression.co.uk. We also have another site for our sister company Hypnotherapy South West which is more to do with me as a therapist practising here in the South West of England. The Association's main site provides information on all aspects of past life therapy with explanations of what the discipline actually is, what it can do and what it feels like. We also have a large online database of therapists so that anyone seeking a regression session can find a practitioner in their locality, both here in the UK and around the world. There is a recommended books section and regression CDs or downloads for sale. And then there is the training school which offers a range of distance learning courses in Past Life Regression and other specialist hypnotherapy techniques. We chose to go the home study route because, not only was there a need, but it was also a good niche to fill. I believe passionately in the way the association trains through our correspondence products and I am sure that, having read the material in this book, you will agree that the need for face to face to tuition in a stuffy classroom is minimal, given the nature of this therapy. In fact, I would go as far as to say that students can benefit from more individual attention from their tutor with our training methods than they would on a residential course with a dozen other students. Distance learning has other benefits too, as it is very cost effective, flexible as far as time is concerned and jolly good for our carbon footprint. The positive comments from our delighted students are testimony to our training methods.

Our most popular course, which we call the Foundation, is designed for anyone who is new to the industry and they can train to become both a

Hypnotherapist and a Past Life Therapist without the need for any previous formal qualifications. Many of our students are now enjoying a new and lucrative career in private practice. So if you fancy a new vocation have a look at our website.

If you are already qualified as a hypnotherapist and have chosen to read this book because you have an interest in past life work, or wish to add this discipline to your existing portfolio of expertise, then we have three past life-based courses especially for you. Our Past Life Regression and Therapy course will qualify you as a Past Life Therapist and can count towards any requirements that you may have for formal ongoing training, known as continuing professional development, or CPD. Once you have completed any of the courses mentioned or have qualified as a Past Life Therapist with another training school then you will be eligible for our flagship Advanced Past Life Regression course. Prior to writing this course much research was undertaken in order to make sure that it became the most thorough and comprehensive work available. It involves the spiritual side and covers many advanced techniques such as Future Life Progression, Life Between Lives, Spirit Release, Soul Retrieval and every other conceivable procedure possible within the framework of past life therapy.

There are other courses as well, two of which are hypnotherapy-based.

All the courses we produce are written in an easy to understand plain English style very much along the lines of the material in this book, big words and unnecessary jargon are definitely excluded. We have trained individuals from all walks of life from all over the world.

There are many books available on the subject of Past Life Regression, some of which you will see advertised on our website and many more in the recommended reading section available for our students. I have worked with various authors on occasions and there is one work in particular that is close to my heart. The book is called My Ever Best Friend by Charles Cane, details of which you can find in the books section on our website. It is a true story and is beautifully written by Charles who, after living with fragmented past life memories for very many years used one of my past life CDs to help him unravel his troubled subconscious. The story that unfolded is very emotional and I could not possibly do it any justice in just a few words here so please find yourself a copy and enjoy. If you have an interest in all things to do with past lives, and in particular Angels, then I would recommend the work by Jenny Smedley, certainly a prolific author and an ambassador for our work. Finally there are two other well-known authors of note, Dr. Brian Weiss, whose books are excellent, and if you're interested in Life Between Lives exploration then the works by Dr. Michael Newton are also a must.

For more information about The Past Life Therapists Association here are some details:

The Past Life Therapists Association
Hypnotherapy South West
Devon
EX21 5EA
United Kingdom

www.pastliferegression.co.uk
www.hypnotherapysouthwest.co.uk

A final thought.

As the year 2012 has come and gone we can prepare ourselves for the evolution which may happen now on a spiritual level.

The general consciousness appears to be to do with change, either negative or positive and there are also a few out there who strongly believed that the end of the world was nigh as we reached the winter solstice of 2012. We're still here.

Collectively, as a species, we can choose to continue as we are and go down the plug hole of greed, hate and selfishness or we can 'raise our vibration' in more positive ways. As stated earlier in this book the planet needs to raise her own vibrational frequency to evolve and survive and it may be our job to help her to do this, first individually and then together, allowing our combined energies to create the conditions for a positive outcome.

And how can we do this? By healing the past. If we lose the baggage from the past and clear the karma then our vibrational frequency will increase.

Past Life Regression will play its part.